THE WINE PIONEERS

By

Anton Massel

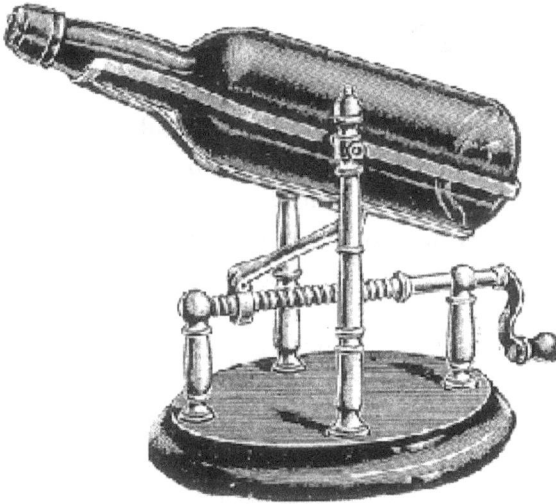

ISBN number: 0-9704932-2-3

THE WINE PIONEERS

By

Anton Massel

ISBN number: 0-9704932-2-3

www.winepioneers.com

It is believed that the information presented in this book is true and accurate at the time of going to press. However, neither the author nor the publisher accepts any legal responsibility or liability for errors, omissions or inaccuracies that may have been made.

Other books by Anton Massel:

Applied Wine Chemistry & Technology
Basic Viticulture
Basic Oenology
Classic Wine Making (with Hugh Barty-King)
Rum - Yesterday and Today (with Hugh Barty-King)

THE WINE PIONEERS

Contents

Part III

Part IV

Introduction

At first there were the horticulturists and wine growers, then came the wine makers, the coopers, and the cellar masters. Inevitably there were wine shippers and wine merchants. Chemists and biologists added their skills in the past two centuries, and only very recently came the oenologists and the professional wine tasters. Wine writers play an important role in today's wine trade, and there were always wine connoisseurs and wine snobs.

Historically progress in perfecting the art of wine making was painfully slow. The first evidence of alcoholic beverages comes from China. Only recently, in 2004 AD, a group of Chinese and American researchers analysed 9000 year old residues of a mixture of fermented rice, honey and fruits, which is currently the oldest evidence of an alcoholic beverage. Records of wine making date from 4000 BC. Interestingly, wine making is a male dominated profession although the first winemaker appears to have been a woman. William Younger reported in his book 'Gods, Men and Wine' (1966) that Siduri, The Wine Maker, is on record of being the first to have made wine from grapes in the 4th millennium BC. No other female winemaker has made the headlines until 1820 when Elizabeth Gervais was granted a patent by Louis XVIII for her invention of an elaborate wine making machine. This interesting detail was recorded by her brother Jean Gervais in 'Opuscule sur la Vinification'. One wonders if women, who were, after all, familiar with household chores, like cooking and preserving food, might not have achieved better results earlier, in terms of wine quality, had they been given the chance.

It is almost impossible to judge the actual quality of the wine that was produced in the early days, but it is more than likely that, to be of drinkable quality, wines would have been very sweet, or with a high degree of alcohol, as otherwise they would have quickly turned to vinegar or suffered other spoilage. In early records we find frequent references that wines were consumed diluted with water, and this explains why. Only fully ripe grapes yield enough sugar to make stable wines. With advanced technology in more recent centuries, it was possible to make quality wines in northern climates from grapes containing moderate amounts of sugar.

The greatest advances in our understanding, and therefore of influencing and controlling wine quality, were made in the 19th century when the French chemist, Luis Pasteur, discovered that micro-organisms are responsible for the alcoholic fermentation and for the fermentations that cause spoilage. Technological advances in the 20th century led to the production of wines of the highest possible quality, but by all accounts, this standard could not be maintained on a broader scale. Commercial considerations such as high yields, the use of oak chips instead of oak casks - to add tannin and flavours - especially to red wines, reverse-osmosis and component separation (alcohol, water and aromas) using high speed centrifuges to change the composition of wine. Sugar additions and measures to make young wines more palatable for early consumption are not conducive either to satisfy the discerning palates. It is therefore all the more important to find wine makers whose integrity is beyond doubt.

By the late 1980s and early 1990s, the discount retailers had so much buying power, that they were in a position to dictate prices to wine growers, with the result, that quality decreased considerably. Numerous wine quality assessments have shown that 10% to 15% of wines on sale in discount stores are not fit for consumption, and a far greater proportion of wine does not entice the would be wine drinker to buy wine again. However, the boom created by the discovery that flavonoids (resveratrol flavonols, anthocyanins, catechins, olgomers) in wine, especially in red wine, are beneficial to health, helped to compensate for the loss of traditional wine drinkers. Good quality wines have become very expensive owing to the high production cost (small crops, oak casks etc.), and the gulf between good and mediocre wines has thus taken on alarming proportions. The losers were the small wine growers and the less affluent consumers but the ´boutique´ wineries are fighting back with innovative methods by making very interesting wines for the interested wine consumers.

Wine fraud has always been a problem and by simply tasting wine it is not possible to identify a tampered wine. The use of methanol to fortify fake wines in Italy, in the late sixties, and the additions of glycol (anti-freeze) to Austrian wines, as recently as 1985, in order to enhance the apparent quality of these wines, are just two examples. Only with the help of chemical analysis could the culprits be convicted.

The new generation of wine makers, who have recognised that integrity is still a virtue, is now set to capture their share of the market.

Acknowledgements

This book resulted from researching a comprehensive amount of literature. Most of the relevant books listed in part IV have been consulted and I am grateful to the authors for providing so much information. Inevitably there have been some books that have been consulted more frequently than others, but the data has been examined for possible variations, and it is almost impossible to single out any books as having been more useful than others. For this reason my thanks go to all the authors, and to the authors of the information I found in the extensive material that is provided by Google and Yahoo.

To my sons Stephen and Mark I am grateful for organising the web-site and having the book printing.

My thanks also go to my wife Doris, for being so understanding because the research has taken more time than it would seem from reading the published material.

Finally, I wish to thank Sandra Spencer, who so patiently checked the m/s and saw to it that my errors were taken care of.

April 2008
Anton Massel

PART I

What is wine, what is wine quality?

The European Economic Community describes wine thus:

"The product derived exclusively from the fermentation or part fermentation of freshly gathered or crushed grapes or the juice of such grapes."

It is generally accepted that wine made from fruit other than grapes is so described, i.e. 'elderberry wine', 'cherry wine' and so on.

The grape is in fact the only fruit, when fully ripe, that provides all the ingredients such as sugar, acids, minerals and colouring matter which are required to make a stable wine of quality, without having to adjust any of the ingredients. This is not to say that there are no variations in its composition and quality depending on the climate, soil, grape variety, microclimate etc. In hot climates grapes can ripen to a greater degree with higher sugar (and therefore higher potential alcohol) and lower acid levels. In less sunny climates the reverse will be the case.

The choice of grape is by far the most important single factor in deciding the type and the quality of wine that is to be produced. It will determine the flavour of the wine and whether it is to be red or white. Some varieties lend themselves to the making of quality, others are for quantity. The choice will depend on market requirements. The ultimate quality, from whatever grape, climate or soil depends on the oenologist - winemaker. Only his or her skill can develop the potential qualities.

Wine quality is subjective. The early wine makers of Mesopotamia, Syria, Egypt, Greece and Italy did not have at their disposal the technical aids we have today and consequently wine consumers appreciated the only wines that could be matured for any length of time before spoilage occurred and these wines had to have sufficient sugar or alcohol to conserve the wine. Later, with the spread of the Roman Empire, the vine came to regions further north, with less favourable climatic conditions, where grapes did not ripen to the same degree and wine makers resorted to fortifying such wines with honey and later with sugar or even distilled alcohol. In years with exceptional sunshine even in northerly regions sound wine could be made without 'improvements' and these wines were and still are of superior quality because the acid-sugar-alcohol balance was perfect. Wine maturation in oak casks, and then in glass bottles sealed with corks, gave another dimension to wine quality which, up to this day, is unsurpassed in good vintages.

Wines that are made from a blend of compatible grape varieties, such as Cabernet Sauvignon, Merlot and Cabernet Frank, as used in Bordeaux, yield wines with outstanding characteristics which are universally appreciated.

Fortified wines such as Sherry, Port, and Madeira are made from a multitude of grape varieties and are fortified with grape distillate (brandy).

Wine growers

Historically it is more than likely that the first cultivators of the vine were horticulturists who have seen wild vines growing up trees and, having tasted the probably poor quality grapes, started to select the best species and planted them in their gardens. Vineyards came much later when the potential of wine making and the pleasures of wine drinking became apparent. Vigneron is the French term used to describe a vineyard worker although in general this is also used to describe a smallholder who grows grapes and makes his own wine. The term ´viticulture´ comes from the Latin name of the plant that produces the best grapes for wine making namely ´Vitis vinifera sativa´ which is the cultivar of the wild ´Vitis vinifera silvestris´.

Of the wine grape, Vitis vinifera sativa, there are today many hundred varieties and the best known wines are made from Chardonnay, Riesling, Sauvignon Blanc, Semillon, Silvaner, Müllet-Thurgau, Muscat, Palomino, Traminer, Chasselas, Chenin Blanc, Veltliner for white wines and Cabernet Sauvignon, Cabernet Franc, Merlot, Pinot Noir, Gamay, Sangiovese, Sirrah (Shiraz) and Nebbiolo for red wines.

In the 19th century the wine blight ´Phylloxera vastatrix´ came to Europe from northern America. This aphid destroyed the European vines (and newly imported Vitis vinifer vines planted in the US) and wine growers had to resort to grafting their vines onto American, Phylloxera resistant root stocks such as Vitis riparia, Vitis rupestris, Vitis berlandieri or crosses of these.

Cultivation techniques have changed during the centuries as can be seen by reading about the achievements of some of the wine pioneers in the following pages.

Coopers

Wine storage and transport vessels have evolved through the centuries. Earthenware containers were probably first used to store wine but they were too heavy for transporting wine long distances. Goat skins became popular for that purpose but the quality of the wine is not likely to have been enhanced.

Coopered containers were first used some 2000 years ago and it was soon learned that wood, especially oak, influenced the wine favourably. Wine alcohol extracts tannins, which improve wine stability, and vanillin considerably improves the flavour. The amounts of tannin and vanillin that are extracted depend on the time the wine remains in the cask and the ratio of wine to wood i.e. a smaller volume of wine has more wood contact surface. Wood is porous and admits small amounts of air (oxygen) which gradually oxidises (matures) the wine without the risk of outright spoilage. Oak also has aseptic properties that counteract, to a limited extent, the activity of spoilage bacteria.

The wine makers of Bordeaux and Burgundy have traditionally the most experience with wine maturation in oak casks. The young wines are stored in a combination of new and used oak casks for periods of up to 30 months, to ensure that the wine extracts just the right amount of oak tannin for their needs. Coopers fashion wooden casks in all shapes and sizes to fit into even the most confined spaces in underground cellars, where wine matures best, and they made large vats for grape must fermentation. One of the most famous wine vats is the Heidelberg tun with a capacity of 227,300 litres (325,000 bottles). It was built in 1751 by Jakob Engler and can be seen at Heidelberg Castle in Germany.

In France, Eugene Mercier of the famous champagne house Mercier, had a tun built which held 140,000 litres (200,000 bottles). It took coopers 20 years to assemble this vast vat, which was built for publicity purposes. It weighed 20 tons and in 1899 it was carted by 24 oxen to Paris for the famous world exhibition. Other more popular and practical sizes are: German stueck, 1200 litres or fuder, 1000 litres; Portuguese pipe, 522 litres; French hogshead or barrique, 225 litres.

In recent decades wine makers, being under commercial pressure and oak barrels being very expensive, add oak shavings, or even worse, pulverised oak to the wine in stainless steel vessels to obtain the oak flavours. However, by this method too much tannin is frequently extracted and the effect of oxygen, as in small cask maturation, is lost. Very often such wines are over-oaked and unpleasant.

Wine-makers

Wine makers are responsible for the production of wine from the time the grapes are ripe and ready to be picked. Wine making is no longer the cottage industry it used to be and most modern wine makers are oenologists with the skills and scientific knowledge taught at universities and higher technical colleges.

Oenologists - Enologists (USA)

Oenology (the science of wine) is a relatively young discipline which began about 100 years ago. The term oenology comes from the Greek 'Oeneus', the legendary King of Calydon. The Greeks described the region of Calabria 'Oenotria' i.e. 'Vineland', when they colonised Sicily and southern parts of Italy from 800 to 700 BC. In their opinion Italy then produced some of the finest wines. Edward Hyams has researched these aspects and reports the results in his book 'Dionysus, A social history of the vine wine´ (1965).

Today there are universities or higher technical colleges with viticulture and wine chemistry research facilities in most wine growing regions and oenologists are graduates of such centers. To study at these facilities students first serve apprenticeships in viticulture and wine making. Oenologists thus have practical experience in wine growing and wine making. In modern wineries they also have at their disposal laboratories to monitor the ripening progress of the grapes so that they can choose the ideal moment for harvesting.

Fermentations are conducted with selected yeast cultures and under controlled temperatures to avoid bacterial spoilage. Wine storage is monitored until the wines are ready for bottling. Bottle maturation, to the point of release, under ideal conditions, is another aspect of successful wine production. Modern installations are complex and require expert supervision of such personnel and for that reason most leading wine makers today are oenologists.

Wine tasters

Wine tasters can be professional people like oenologists, wine makers, wine merchants, wine buyers, sommeliers or wine writers, or they can be amateurs such as wine lovers, wine connoisseurs or even wine snobs.

The professional wine taster will be engaged full time in the trade with appropriate training. Wine tasting can be arranged as ´horizontal´ tasting, i.e. wines of the same vintage are compared with samples of wines from different estates or countries or wines of the same vintage made from different vine varieties. In ´vertical´ tasting wines from successive vintages from a single estate, region or country are assessed.

One of the first official wine tasters was appointed by the South African government in 1811, to ensure that the wines exported to Britain were sound and not less than eighteen months old, so that their reputation was maintained at a high level. This 'Wine Taster's Office' was abolished in 1826.

Wine tasting or degustation is technically an organoleptic examination of representative samples of wines using the senses sight, smell and taste. The greatest asset of a wine taster, apart from a good nose and palate, is a good memory, to be able to accumulate impressions from past tasting, so that this data can be recalled for comparison. The opinion expressed by a single taster, however, can be no more than his or her personal opinion even though it may be an 'expert' opinion. Opinions which carry much more weight are those of a panel of tasters and for this reason wine buyers engage more people to express their impressions before decisions are taken.

A further limitation for organoleptic examinations is the inability of our senses to identify the origins of various substances such as alcohols, tannins, flavours, glycerine and the scandalous glycol. Another handicap is the susceptibility of our mind.

A French research team under Frédéric Brochet has provided proof that the well known psychological phenomenon – you taste what you are expected to taste – is valid. He invited 54 of Bordeaux's eminent wine tasters to sample different wines, including a white wine to which he added a flavourless red colour. Not a single taster noticed that it was not a red wine. What we perceive, says M. Brochet, is a mixture of thought, vision and taste. Indeed, the brain receives more information from the eyes than from the mouth or nose. In other words, a single opinion is for practical purposes only good for the taster himself. It is useless as a guide for others. The average opinion of a group of tasters, as many as possible, and not just 'experts', who have pre-conceived ideas, is worth having.

So where does this leave the oenologist who sends his wines to be judged by wine tasters like wine writers, who can make or break his reputation, when their verdicts are published? Sadly, these people are so busy, they tend to taste hundreds of wines daily, with the result that many a fine wine 'goes under' because delicate flavours go unnoticed in tasting which include 'big wines'. Modern jargon describes such wines as 'concentrated'. To save their reputation, wine makers must produce and submit 'concentrated' wines for their scrutiny, although they know that too much alcohol, tannin, extract, colour and flavour do not necessarily make a ´fine´ wine.

The above makes it quite clear that, in order to evaluate wines objectively, it is absolutely necessary to engage a group of tasters and that the samples are presented without displaying the labels or disclosing the price. More than 25 to 30 samples in one tasting session also make it difficult to appreciate the finer bouquet and flavours when the senses have become 'dulled' by the alcohol, even if the famous spitting technique is practiced.

Masters of wine

Masters of Wine are essentially professional wine tasters.

In 1953 the Wine and Spirit Association of Great Britain and the Vintners' Company started study sessions covering all aspects of the wine and spirits trade, with particular emphasis in wine tasting. Successful candidates qualified for membership of the Institute of Masters of Wine (MW).

In 1968 the Wine & Spirit Education Trust was added to the educational facilities for all members of the trade. Before candidates can take the MW exam they must have successfully completed the Wine and Spirit Education Trust Certificate and Diploma courses.

In the UK many Masters of Wine are wine buyers.

Vintners´

Vintners´are wine merchants, but not all wine merchants are Vintners´, because this title is reserved for members of the Vintners´ Company.

The Vintners´ Company is one of the ancient Livery Companies of the City of London dating back to 1364. Its wealth and influence resulted from the rich wine merchants, its members. The Vintners´ effectively controlled the British wine trade for several centuries and due to its success the fraternity purchased a grant of incorporation in 1437 and the Company thus became a legal entity.

Curiously, apart from furthering the educational facilities of the wine trade, the Vintners´ Company, to this day, provides the ´Swan Warden´ who is responsible for these protected birds living on the river Thames.

Anne Crawford has recorded the history and activities of the Vintners´ Company in her book ´A History of the Vintners´ Company´ (1977).

Wine shippers/Wine merchants

The Greeks and Romans shipped their wines across the Mediterranean sea and later, on rivers like the Garonne, Rhone, Loire, Moselle and the Rhine, to destinations in northern Europe.

Retail wine merchants distributed the wines locally to their customers. Later, enterprising merchants traveled to the wine growing regions to select wines with their customer's preferences in mind. In England, wine merchants like Berry Brothers and Rudd, Avery's of Bristol, Harveys of Bristol and many more became famous.

Some of the shippers discovered that wines, like Madeira, improved on long sea voyages, but many other wines could not be brought to their destination without deteriorating en route. Many a wine shipper thus settled in countries like Spain (Jerez or Malaga) and Portugal (Oporto) to modify wine making techniques so that these wines could be shipped safely. That way fortified wines were created which to this day have a strong following in many countries.

In modern times wine businesses have become international conglomerates who can also be vineyard owners. They combine wine production, shipping and retailing. Even supermarkets ship some of their own wines.

Sommeliers/Wine waiters

Sommelier is the French name for a wine waiter who serves wines in restaurants. In better restaurants wine waiters are generally referred to as sommeliers and they are expected to know all about the wines that restaurant stocks. Sadly, not all the sommeliers are well informed and frequently they can be intimidating with the little knowledge they have. Connoisseurs are well advised to learn all they can about the better, more expensive wines, so that they can judge the ability of such wine waiters before accepting their advice.

In recent decades, efforts have been made to educate serious sommeliers and the chances that we meet a knowledgeable waiter are rising. This is a welcome development because a person who has the opportunity of frequently tasting the quality wines of his well stocked cellar is in a better position to tell when an especially good vintage is ready for drinking. The choice of wine is, after all, frequently the key to a successful and enjoyable event.

The training of a sommelier also includes the storage and serving of wine. Needless to say, wine should be stored at the constant temperature of 14 to 16° C.

The serving temperature depends on the type of wine. Champagne and sweet white wine at about 8° C, dry white wine at 10° C, and very young red wine can be served at cellar temperature (16° C). They should be decanted an hour or two before serving to enhance, with air contact, the flavours. Mature red wines with natural deposits of tartrates and colouring matter must be decanted to separate the deposit, but air contact should be limited to a short period to avoid undue oxidation of the rather delicate flavours and loss of the irreplaceable volatile bouquet fractions. Such fine wines should be served at room temperature of about 20° C. On very hot days with ambient temperatures rising to more than 30° C. it is not advisable to drink these exceptional, mature and frequently expensive wines because it is unlikely that their potential can be fully appreciated.

Wine connoisseurs, wine snobs and wine lovers.

Connoisseurs are wine lovers who are genuinely interested in wine and who are keen to learn all they can about the subject but do not have the opportunity to be involved professionally.

Wine snobs are people with little knowledge who do not express their own opinion but have much to say about the many great vintages they have tasted. The knowledge and information, which they are only too keen to pass on in a boring fashion, is gleaned from others. Unfortunately, very often, genuine wine lovers are placed in the category of the wine snob.

To avoid being tarred with that brush, it is best for genuine connoisseurs to wait until an opinion is asked for and then to give a brief account of impressions making it quite clear that this is a personal opinion which may well not be shared by others present.

True connoisseurs consider eating and drinking a part of culture. Combining the right wine with the flavours of good food is indeed an art which few people can master.

Wine writers

Alcuin (735-804 A.D.), a Yorkshireman who was appointed tutor to the Imperial court of Charlemagne, is on record of having given written instructions to his suppliers on how the wines he ordered should be handled. Pamela Vandyke-Price, a prolific wine writer herself, stated in her book 'A Taste of Wine' (1975) that Alcuin was the first known person to write about wines.

However, Cato (234 to 149 B.C.), in his 'De Agricultura', listed in great detail how vineyards and wineries are to be established and at what cost. Varro (116 to 27 B.C.) wrote in similar terms and Pliny, in the first century A.D., was even more prolific. He devoted a whole book to wine in his 'Natural History', giving details on how vines were pruned and trained and he published long lists of grape varieties with size, shape, colour, taste and what they were good for.

Around 65 A.D. Lucius Columilla, the Gades (Cadiz) born agronomist and viticulturist, was by far the most scientific Roman writer with precise reports in twelve volumes of his 'De La Rustica'. He wrote on how to plant vineyards commercially and how to treat wines.

Ausonius, around 379 A.D., published his 'Moselle' in which he described the Moselle vineyards, which were already of commercial importance.

In ca. 400 A.D. Palladius provided written instructions to the Greeks on how to improve the flavour, colour, and strength of their wines and to give to new wine the quality of old wine. He says for example: "one so effectually useful to this purpose, that it was said to be communicating to the Cretans by the Pythean oracle; in which, among other ingredients, the hepatic loess has a considerable share" (Lib. XI. De Re Rustica).

Arnaldus de Ville, a physician, surgeon and alchemist published the first wine book, handwritten around 1310 (Gutenberg had not yet invented the printing press). In 1478 it was translated and printed in German. An English version was published in 1943.

One of the first English educational text-books, with valuable information for wine connoisseurs and thus promoting wine consumption, 'In Vino Veritas', was written by André L Simon in 1913. This book, and its companion, 'The Blood of the Grape' (1920), were sponsored by London's ´Wine Trade Club´. André Simon has written more than a hundred other books, mainly on wine, in his long life and at the age of 92, a year before he passed away and with his eyesight fading, he typed for me the following notes about his life:

"Planning had little to do - I might even say nothing to do - with my life. But providence certainly looked after me!

My father had a seaside house in Normandy, where we spent some time every summer from Paris. In 1894, my father suggested that I might go to Southampton from St. Malo and spend a month or six weeks in England and improve my knowledge of English. I accepted his offer with joy, and that is how I happened to meet, in Southampton, in August 1894, a charming 15 year old English girl. I was seventeen. We were married in 1900, and she left me to go to heaven in 1963.
No planning.

In 1895, my father died suddenly at 47. One of his wartime (1870-7) friends, the Marques de Polignac, had married the only daughter of the wealthy widow Pommery of Champagne fame. He asked my mother if he could be of any use to her getting a job for one or two of her sons – there were six of them – in the Champagne Pommery firm and that is how the best 33 years of my life were spent in the wine trade with headquarters in Mark Lane, London. No planning!

In 1903, talking to A. S. Gardiner, the then editor of Wine & Spirit Trade Review, over a glass of Champagne, I casually remarked that had it not been for a chance visit to Southampton, in 1894, I would not have been selling Champagne in England, but writing for Le Figaro and other newspapers in Paris; writing had been my first ambition, and, I believed, my vocation. "If that is so, said Gardiner, you will never be happy unless you write, and I am sure that you will find it possible to write, as well, about Champagne!" That may be, but what would be the use? I have no contacts now in the Paris Press, nor anything to write about; and nobody over here could possibly be interested in anything I might attempt to write in English. "You are quite wrong," said Gardiner, "and to prove it to you I commission you, here and now, to write twelve articles on Champagne which I will publish in the Wine & Spirit Trade Review, to be paid for at the usual rate".
Twelve articles! I cold write one, I thought, on the vineyards, rivers, cities and villages of Champagne. I could write a chapter on the making of Champagne but that was all I knew. When and how was Champagne first introduced in England? How and why it became fashionable? I would dearly have loved to know the answer to these and to many other such questions. Thanks to Gardiner who introduced me to the Librarian of the Guildhall Library, and who told me how to get a readers card for the British Museum, I found the answers I wanted.

The Wine & Spirit Trade Review had my twelve articles by 1904, and they were published, in 1905, in book form as 'A HISTORY OF THE CHAMPAGNE TRADE IN ENGLAND', the first of my many books."
André L. Simon

Hugh Johnson is, today, probably the best known wine writer. His many editions of 'The World Atlas of Wine' (first published in 1971), are a huge success. Jancis Robinson MW is equally successful with 30 years of writing about wine and with many books to her credit. Robert M. Parker, who published the results of scores of wine tasting in his 'The Wine Advocate', is probably the favourite author for the Americans.

There are, of course, hundreds of wine writers, all experts in their chosen professions. Most newspapers have wine writers on their staff and they use the most florid language to describe the wines that are offered at the many trade tastings. However, the days have gone when authors like James Thurber have given us lines like: "a naïve little Burgundy which he hoped that we would be amused by its presumption". Or, when Stephen Potter spoke of: "The imperial decay of his invalid port, its gracious withdrawal from perfection keeping a hint of former majesty withal as it hovered between oblivion and the divine 'untergang' of infinite recession".

Today's wine descriptions are more in line with: "it is goaty, meaty or it has an aroma of tobacco, licorice, fish, geranium, or even farm yard". These descriptions do not encourage would be wine drinkers to buy wine and when they are offered immature, over-oaked produce it is no wonder that we now have a generation of wine drinkers without ambitions to improve their knowledge of wine.

Many a wine grower and winemaker has put pen to paper to write informative books on interesting wine topics and in my book 'Applied Wine Chemistry and Technology' (1969), I had published a comprehensive bibliography . For twenty five years, until the late 1980's, I have handled, through my 'Wine Book Club', thousands of titles and in part IV of this book I have provided an up-dated version of this bibliography which now reads a bit like who's who in the wine trade. I have listed only books published in English before 1990.

Of course, such lists can never be complete, but I have included, after all, 1500 or so names of wine experts who have shared the information they have gathered for us. They should not be forgotten in a book of this nature.

Part II

The wine pioneers - Chronological index

There are many more notable wine growers, wine makers, merchants and oenologists worthy of being listed in this book.

4000 BC	Siduri. She is the first winemaker on record.
2337 BC	Noah, it is claimed by a German historian, has planted the first vine and is thus given credit for being the father of viticulture.
1300 BC	Khaa, Tutankhamun´s winemaker.
65AD	L.J.M Columella, the leading agronomist of his time, published works on general farming, viticulture and dendrology and must indeed be the first known wine writer of repute.
92	Domitian ordered the destruction of transalpine vineyards.
280	Emperor Probus lifted the vine planting ban imposed by Domitian.
812	The Emperor Charlemagne (742- 814), considered to be the father of Europe, actively promoted viticulture.
1151	Hildegard of Bingen, the Abbess of the monasteries Disibodenberg and Rupertsberg (Germany) in her ´Causa et Curae´, recommends undernourished people to eat moderately fat meat and to drink a glass of wine. She also advises "discretio" - moderate alcohol consumption is wholesome.
1211	The Knights of Greiffenclau produced their first wine at Schloss Vollrads, Winkel

(Rheingau), and to this day the estate makes top quality wines, although Erwein Graf Matuschka-Greiffenclau, who managed the estate from 1975, committed suicide in the early 1990's.

1358   Dr. Albucasis, Arnold de Villeneuf and Ortholaus are the pioneers of wine distillation and rectification.

1590   The Jesuit monks brought European vine seeds to Baja California to grow grapes and to make communion wine.

1668   Dom Perignon, the famous French winemaker, was appointed cellarer of the Benedictine Abbey at Haut Villier near Epernay, and perfected the art of Champagne making.

1729   Nicolas Ruinart is on record of being the first Champagne shipper.

1730   The Domecq bodegas date back to 1730 but their fame started with Don Pedro Domecq.

1743   Claude Moét founded the company that is now the largest Champagne house, 'Moét et Chandon'.

1771   Fra. Junipero Serra brought vitis Vinifera vine cuttings (known as 'Mission vine') to northern California. He founded the 'Mission San Gabriel', and there he built his winery which is the oldest in north America. The Franciscans were the only noteworthy wine growers in northern California.

1788   Captain Arthur Phillip, R.N. disembarked with his cargo of convicts, free men and vines. By 1791, he was then Governor of

	Australia, he had planted a three acre vineyard at the Government House property.
1790	William Speechley, the Duke of Portland's, gardener, is on record of being first to deliberately cross-pollinate vines to produce new varieties.
1791	Phillip Schaffer, a German emigrant, planted a one acre vineyard on the banks of the Parramatta river, New South Wales, and this has been recognised as the first private commercial vineyard of Australia.
1799	Nicole-Barbe Ponsardin married Fransçois Cliquot. She later founded Veuve Cliquot-Ponsardin and, with Edouard Werlé, invented the pupitre table.
1800	Le Compte Chaptal published his book 'L'Arte de Faires les Vins', in which he described the "art of improving low quality grape must" in France.
1816	Andreas Jordan is considered the founder of quality viticulture in the Palatinate, Germany, and Dr. H.C Friedrich von Bassermann-Jordan is the author of the definitive work on the history of viticulture.
1819	Samuel Marsden planted the first vine cuttings in New Zealand's North Island.
1820	Elizabeth Gervais invented a wine making machine to improve the quality of her wines for which Louis XVIII granted her a patent.
1825	James Busby brought vine cuttings to Australia, and in 1833 he also planted the first vineyard in New Zealand.
1830	Jean Luis Vignes brought 'noble' vine cuttings from Cadillac (France) to 'El Pueblo de Nuestro Señora la Reina de Los Angeles de Porciuncula', today's Los

	Angeles. He changed his name and became famous as 'Don Luis'.
1830	Around this time Juan Sanchez, son of a well to do Santander family, came to Jerez, Spain and became a famous and probably the first roving winemaker.
1831	Joseph James Forrester (Baron de Forrester) came to Oporto in 1831 and became a leading protector of Port wine.
1833	Manuel Maria Gonzalez Angel established one of the most powerful Sherry dynasties still known as 'Gonzales Byass & Co'. Threir most famous brand is the Tio Pepe Fino Sherry.
1836	Romero (General) Vallejo was the last Mexican military commandant of Sonoma, California who founded the town of Sonoma, and later established his own vineyard, 'Lachrima Montis', in Sonoma County.
1849	Ephram Bull of Concord, Massachusetts, introduced the 'Concord' vine which has become the leading grape variety for sweet wine production in the eastern USA.
1849	Agoston Haraszthy came to Sonoma and founded the 'Buena Vista Winery'. He shipped more than 100.000 cuttings of Vitis vinifera varieties from Europe and became known as the 'Father of modern California wine'.
1850	Don Camilo de Amézaga, Marqués de Riscal, founded what is now the oldest and one the best known bodegas in Rioja, Spain.
1850	Thomas Hardy shipped the first commercial quantity (2 hogsheads) of Australian wine to England from his vineyard on the river

	Torrens. He was the only Austrailian winemaker who was honoured with a memorial.
1858	Charles Krug, a German pioneer, established the first commercial California (Napa Valley) winery and made a name for himself as a fine winemaker.
1860	Louis Pasteur, the French scientist discovered about this time that micro-organisms are responsible for fermentations.
1860	Freiherr von Babo, a pioneer in viticulture and wine making and a prolific author, founded the private Weinbauschule at Chorherrenstift, Klosterneuburg, Austria.
1865	Jules Guyot, the French scientist, introduced his system of vine pruning for trellises and advised on how to produce quality wines.
1866	Benno Seppelt was the architect of the Seppelt dynasty, one of the earliest and largest wine businesses in Australia.
1870	George Husmann, Professor of Horticulture at the University of Missouri, was one of the first to see the benefit of gafting Euopean vine cuttings onto American, Phylloxera resistant, rootstocks to save viticulture from ruin.
1872	Barone Bettino Ricasoli was essentially the father of Chianti Classico.
1872	José Raventos made the first Spanish sparkling wine, now called Cava, and thus founded what became the world's largest sparkling wine producer.
1880	Eugene Hilgard established the Agricultural Experiment Station and started to classify the wine regions of California by ´degree days´.

1882	H. Müller (Thurgau) was a vine breeder and it is thought that with the crossing Riesling and Silvaner he created the Müller-Thurgau, one of the most widely planted varieties in Germany.
1883	Melchor de Concha y Toro has pioneered classic wine making in Chile.
1890	Charles William Henry Kohler was the founder of the Ko-operatieve Wijnbouwers Vereniging (KWV) and is considered one of the most honoured figures of South Africa's successful wine industry.
1891	Theobald Friedrich Seitz invented the first wine filter which revolutionised wine making and wine marketing.
1895	Romeo Bragato, a viticultural expert, was appointed advisor to the Governor of New Zealand. He chose Tekawhata as the best climatic site where he established the first 'Vine Research Station'.
1896	Francis Lawrence Berry, Charles Walter Berry, and later Major Hugh Rudd, of Berry Brothers & Co. made 'Number Three St. James's Street', London, the most envied address of the wine world.
1897	M. Crétien Oberlin discovered the Gewuerztraminer which made, with Riesling, the wines of Alsace famous.
1900	Julius Wegeler bought a part of Gemany's most famous vineyard, the 'Bernkasteler Doktor', for a record sum of 100 gold marks.
1902	Frédéric Emile Hugel pioneered the re-emergence of Alsace as a quality wine producer after the ravages of Phylloxera, Oidium, Peronospera and World War I.

1902	Assid Abraham Corban came to New Zealand via Australia and founded what is now the oldest and most successful NZ wine business.
1911	Rudolf Jordan Jr. is one of the first wine makers to advocate cold fermentation for Californian white wine.
1916	Friedrich Schmitthenner invented a new filter that removes from wine unwanted yeast and bacteria. This revolutionised wine bottling and marketing.
1920	Henri Gauge, together with the Marquis d´Angerville, was a true pioneers in the fight against fraud in Burgundy during the 1920s
1919	Henri Woltner bought ´Ch. La Mission Haut-Brion´, and with his skills as a winemaker made the estate famous.
1922	Baron Phillipe de Rothschild, at age 20, was put in charge of the then "old forgotten farm" of Chateau Mouton.
1922	Louis M. Martini Sr. has been the patriarch of the modern California wine industry.
1923	Wilhelm Möslinger, a German wine chemist, developed ´blue fining´ a treatment that removes excess iron and copper from contaminated wine. It is the only treatment that ensures stability of such wines.
1924	Albert Bürklin managed the Weingut Dr. Bürklin-Wolf, the largest private wine estate in Germany for five decades and left an astonishing heritage.
1930	Max Chaputier came into the family business about this time at the age of 23 to run the company, and at the same time

helped Rhone wines to the success they enjoy today.

1932   Maynard A. Amerine was California's foremost scientist on enology and viticulture.

1933   Leon D. Adams founded the Grape Growers League of California/Wine Institute.

1933   Earnest and Julio Gallo founded what has become the world's largest wine empire.

1934   Harry Waugh was considered to have one of the best palates in the wine trade. He became a director of chateau Latour and wine consultant to HM Queen Elizabeth II.

1934   Georges Faiveley and Camille Rodier founded the famous wine fraternity ´La Confrerie des Chevalier du Tastevin´ to promote the wines of Burgundy.

1934   Erwin Wanner developed controlled fermentation and the Geisenheim- Viewing-Cask (oak cask with glass ends).

1935   Brother Timothy bacame cellar master at the Christian Brothers when they started their activities in the Napa Valley. At the famous ´Mont La Salle´ vineyard, extending to 360 acres, he produced the legendary ´Pineau de la Loire´ (Chenin Blanc) wine.

1937   Gerhard Troost was an oenologist in every sense of the word.

1938   André Tschelinstcheff, a Russian wine expert, brings Beaulieu Vinayards to prominence and earns himself the title ´Dean of California Winemakers´.

1940   Lenz Moser introduced in Austria his high culture system for viticulture.

1942   Paul Alfons Fürst von Metternich, the present owner of the famous

	Sckloss Vollrads, Johannisberg in the Rheingau, faced the Herculian task of re-building the estate after it was bombed in 1942.
1944	Joseph Heitz arrived in California and became one of Californias best known wine makers.
1950	Alexis Lichine, a chateau owner, winemaker, merchandiser and author did much to promote wine, especially in the US.
1950	Miguel Torres and his son Miguel Agustin Torres pioneered the modern Spanish wine industry by planting classic French and German grape varieties, introducing new vine training systems and using cold fermentation techniques in stainless steel tanks.
1950	The Marquis de Goulaine, one of the leading wine growers of Muscadet, France set high quality standards for the dry and crisp Loire wines which became so popular.
1950	Wilhelm Geiss developed cold sterile wine bottling.
1952	Sir Guy Salisbury-Jones GCVO, CMG, CBE, MC led the revival of English viticulture by planting the first commercial vineyard, and in 1967 he became the first president of the newly formed ´English Vineyards Association´.
1953	Max Schubert re-invented Australian red wine making. He made the first vintage of the now famous Penfolds ´Grange Hermitage´.
1956	Pierre Galet identified vine varieties for the first time by observing vine leaves and not relying on the inexact comparison of fruit

clusters as did his predecessors. He published his comprehensive 'Ampelography' between 1956 and 1964.

1958   Miljenko Grgich, the Croation oenologist, produced the wine at Chateau Montelina, Napa Valley, which was judged best Chardonnay at the famous 1976 French/Calfornia tasting in Paris.

1961   Wolf Blass arrived in Australia, and with his skills as a winemaker and showman he achieved fame and fortune within three decades.

1963   Max Lake planted his 'Lake's Folly' vineyard in the Hunter Valley, New South Wales, Australia.

1964   Warren Winiarsky and his wife Barbara came to California to start their new vocation as wine growers and wine makers, and in 1976 their '1973 Stag's Leap Cabernet Sauvignon' won first prize in the famous Paris tasting.

1964   Alan Rook planted the worlds most northerly Vinyard.

1966   Michael Broadbent, one of the first Masters of Wine, joined Christie's to re-start their wine auctions.

1966   Hans Ambrosi, oenologist and prolific wine writer, brings fame to the Staatsdomäne Kloster Eberbach, Rheingau.

1966   Robert Mondavi started his own, now famous, winery in Oakville, Napa Valley, California.

1968   Giacomo Tachis is considered one of the best wine makers of Italy who introduced the Cabernet Sauvignon to Tuscany. As

	winemaker to Antinori he produced the famous 'Tignanello'.
1968	Marchese Piero Antinori, the present head of the Antinori wine estates made history when he introduced Cabernet Sauvignon and other classic grape varieties to his 'cépage', against the establishment governing Chianti production.
1970	Richard Peterson is probably America's most innovative enologists.
1976	Stephen Spurrier organised the famous Paris tasting of California v. French Chardonnay and Cabernet Sauvignon wines. This has put the spotlight on the wines of California.

Part III

The wine pioneers - Chronologically

5000 BC to 753 BC

Alcoholic fermentation, undoubtedly, occurred accidentally long before any records were kept. It is likely, that diluted honey or forgotten residues of fruit juices fermented, and resulted in an intoxicating, alcoholic beverage that will have amused many of our ancestors once it was discovered that such liquids did not do lasting damage. It is impossible to date this event. However, grape wine can be traced along the path grape cultivation has taken. Serious wine making was only possible with grape juice because the grape is the only fruit that contains enough natural sugar to yield a wine with sufficient alcohol to remain drinkable for any length of time before spoilage begins.

Vitis vinifera silvestris has grown in the wild since pre-historic times. First evidence has been found in the tertiary layers of the earth's crust (60 million to 1 million years old) in many parts of the world. Vitis vinifera sativa, a cultivar of silvestris, our wine grape, heralded the beginning of the ancient art of vine cultivation and wine making as we know it.

Siduri the winemaker

It is thought that the first vine cultivars came from Armenia, but the Sumerians and Egyptians planted vineyards from 5000 to 3000 B.C., and the first records of wine making were found in royal tombs dating back to 2780 B.C. Jars of wine were provided for the dead rulers to refresh themselves during their travels in the next world.

Siduri, the Maker of Wine (or Goddess?), but certainly immortal, is mentioned in the 'Epic of Gilgamish' from the 4th Millennium B.C. She was probably the first winemaker. The UR texts, among the earliest agricultural documents in the world, also point to Babylon as being the cradle of viticulture and wine making, although it is known, that in the Sumerian civilisation in Mesopotamia beer brewed from barley was the national drink.

Noah

The legend goes (and the German historian Dr. R. Haas claims in his book ´Rheingauer Geschichts- und Wein-Chronik´, dated 1854 that Noah planted the first vine in 2337 B.C.

"And Noah he said to his wife when he sat down to dine:
I don't care where the water goes, if it doesn't get into the wine".
G.K.Chesterton.

Khaa, Tutankhamun's winemaker

Syrian wine was found in refrigerated chambers at the palace of ´Mari of Hammurabi´, the unifier of Babylonia (1793-1750 B.C.). The wines must have been good, because the Egyptians had brought cuttings from that country to improve their own stock. Rosa Lamuela-Raventos and her research team at the University of Barcelona (Spain), have recently examined wine residues found in jars from the tomb of King Tutankhamun who reigned in the 1300´s B.C. The chemical analysis (liquid chromatography and mass spectrometry) revealed that the wine was made from red grapes. The winemaker's name, Khaa, is inscribed on the jars which can be seen at the

British Museum in London and the Egyptian Museum in Cairo.

The terms oinos, yayin, tirosh, debhash and schechar were used freely to describe wines made from all kinds of fruit or honey to which sometimes spices were added for flavour and to conserve the wines. The Greek oinos was later widely used for wines made exclusively from grapes.

The grapes that were harvested for those early wine makers are likely to have been similar in quality to present day crops in the same climatic environments, but the resultant wines would have been quite different. The naturally occurring yeast strains were undoubtedly less efficient than the selected yeast cultures of today; they would not have been able to ferment high degrees of alcohol from the available sugar and consequently many wines will have been only partly fermented, i.e. some sugar remained unfermented.

Low alcohol content implies that the wines will have been liable to attack by bacteria capable of converting alcohol to vinegar. Oxidation through lack of effectively sealed storage containers will have produced off flavours and led to general deterioration. Only wines made from grapes with exceptionally high sugar contents, which were protected by the alcohol and a high concentration of residual grape sugar (sugar exerts osmotic pressure on microorganisms thus arresting their activity), could be stored and matured for any length of time. These were the wines that lasted for reportedly one or two hundred years and were much appreciated by their proud owners.

From our perspective it is not surprising, therefore, that these early wines, young or old, were consumed diluted with water, because they would have been too sweet or they would have had very intensive flavours, good or bad.

753 BC - 476 AD

Viticulture saw the greatest expansion during the over a thousand years of the Roman Empire which started with the founding of Rome in 753 B.C. and its collapse in the west 476 A.D.

The Phoenicians (the then Lebanon), brought Vitis vinifera vines to the European continent from their country, via Minoan Crete to Greece, and from Egypt came the art of wine making. In Homer's time, about 700 B.C., vine culture was well established and wine had become part of the staple diet of the Greeks who served it at breakfast time soaked in bread.

The Geek philosopher Epicurus (342-270 B.C.), the founder of the Epicurian school, enjoyed wine in full measure and Pliny reported that the same grape could produce different wines under different conditions, and that soil and climate had a profound effect on quality. Pliny devoted a whole book to the subject wine in his ´Natural History´ (1st century A.D.), and in his fourteenth book he warned that the dangers of alcohol were profound. The Romans already knew how to avoid wine turning to vinegar and that some wines improved in time when stored correctly.

Apicius, an extravagant cook and gourmand (sic), wrote a cookery book in the 1st century A.D. in which he gave many recipies using herbs and flavoured wines for his sauces. He favoured sweet/sour dishes which are thought to help the metabolism of fat. This and other reports give us the idea that Roman wines were not as pure as our wines today. Most wines were in fact adulterated with honey, herbs, additions of various (dried) fruits, resins and even sea water to make poor wines more palatable (sweeter).

Later, with micro-climatic conditions being suitable, vineyards were planted in Sicily, Sardinia, Carthage, Gades (Cadiz) and other Phoenician communities. Within a few centuries vineyards appeared in southern Italy and southern France (Massalia/ Marseilles). From Spain the vine reached Portugal.

The Phoenicians were defeated by the Romans at Carthage in 146 B.C. and Egypt was conquered in 30 B.C. The wines of the Roman territories thus became popular and were appreciated in other parts of their empire throughout their reign and beyond. This is especially true for the Falernian (Campania) wines.

Lucius Junius Moderatus Columella

Columilla was an agronomist born in Cadiz during the reign of Augustus. As early as 65 A.D. he meticulously reported his scientific discoveries on agriculture and dendrology. In regard to viticulture and wine making he recommended, for example, the sprinkling of Gypsum (calcium sulphate) in the Jerez vineyards onto grapes before they were pressed to increase the tartaric acid content in the wine. This is still common practiced today. He gave detailed instructions on how and when to plant vines and he warned of possible financial losses under given circumstances etc. Columella was a scientist of note and the published information was precise.

The Emperors Domitian and Probus

Civilisation reached the northern parts of Europe from Greece via Italy, Gaul, Germany and eventually Britain.

Wine was accepted as the civilised beverage, but only the ruling classes could afford the valued Greek and Latium imports. The Roman Emperors motivated their soldiers with wine, which was therefore of paramount importance to them and since logistics were not as they are today it was difficult to meet demand. The soldiers soon planted vines and made wine in the countries they occupied. The second ally of the vine was the clergy. Monasteries needed sacramental wines and so did the monks. The Vineyards flourished to such an extent, that in 90 A.D. the Emperor Domitian forbade the planting of vines; indeed he ordered that existing vineyards be uprooted so that grain and other crops could be grown instead to feed the starving population. In 280 A.D. the Emperor Probus lifted the ban and vineyards were planted again. However, quality and yields could not at this time compete with imported wines, and viticulture in northern Europe was thus limited to only the most favourite sites.

476 B.C. - 1800 A.D.

With the disintegration of the Roman Empire around 476
A.D. viticulture greatly decreased and a revival was only
evident from the time of the Emperor Charlemagne's reign
(742 A.D. - 814 A.D.). Later, during the reign of Otto the
Great (936 A.D. - 973 A.D.), the first grape presses were
invented and this heralded a new approach to wine making
with better quality. The old controversies on how wine
should be preserved, how to make it seaworthy for
transport by water, whether air was a friend or foe during
the fermentation, whether the stalks should be removed or
fermented with the berries and at what point, if any, the
fermentation should be stopped were topics again. For
centuries many of these points could not be fully answered
until Louis Pasteur discovered, around 1860, that micro-
organisms were responsible for fermentations.

The Emperor Charlemagne

No other part of the world produces better Riesling wines
than the Rheingau. The first vineyards were most likely
planted there as early as 810.

A Rhineland legend tells of Charlemagne, who frequently
stayed at his residence in Ingelheim on the left bank of the
Rhine. He noticed that in the spring the snow on the slopes
on the other side of the Rhine, near the present Schloss
Johannisberg estate, was melting when other parts were
still white and cold. He promptly ordered that a vineyard to
be planted there and this produced excellent wine.

This is probably true, because Charlemagne's son, Ludwig,
recorded a harvest of 6 Fuder (6000 litres) wine in 817.
Charlemagne passed laws for the protection of viticulture

and, as Alfred Langenbach put it in his book 'The Wines of Germany' (1951): "Of all, the Frankish dynasty is rightly credited; one of the most praiseworthy is the attempt to foster viticulture in the Rheingau".

An event of great historical importance illustrates the value attached to viticulture. Only three decades after the death of Charlemagne the three Frankish Kings met at Verdun in 843 to divide the Empire, and viticulture was considered a valued asset. This was stated in the 'Chronicum Reginonis' report.

The white Riesling grape, known in California as the Johannisberg Riesling, grown in the Rheingau on slate and loess soil, yields small crops but outstanding wines with rich, concentrated fruit flavours and good, crisp acidity. It is the acidity that makes them mature extremely long and well. Most of the better wines need three to four years maturation in bottle. The 'Beerenauslese' and 'Trockenbeerenauslese' wines last for a century or more.

Hildegard of Bingen

In 1151 Hildegard of Bingen, Abbess of the Monasteries of Disbodenberg and Rupertsberg (Germany), began her 'Causa et Curae', the book on natural medicines in which wine features on numerous occasions. For patients with angina pectoris and heart failure she prescribed her 'heart wine' which consisted of good wine, fresh parsley stems and honey. In one passage she recommends undernourished people to "eat moderately fat meat and to drink a glass of wine". She also advises "discreto"; only moderate alcohol consumption is wholesome.

The Knights of Greiffenclau

The Knights of Greiffenclau have produced wine at Schloss Vollrads, Winkel in the Rheingau from 1211. Records show that they have supplied wines to the Monastery of St. Victor in Mainz at that time.

In 1846 Graf Hugo Matuschka married a niece of the last Greiffenclau and the name was thus changed to Matuschka-Greiffenclau. The family has carried on the tradition of wine making and direct marketing exclusively from the Riesling grape with distinction, and the last but one owner Graf Richard Matuschka-Greiffenclau has devoted his life to viticulture. He was for many years President of the 'German Wine Growers Federation', German delegate to the "International Wine Council' in Paris, Chairman of the 'Agricultural Co-operative Federation' in Frankfurt, a Director of the 'Teaching and Research Institute' at Geisenheim and a member of the Presidential Committee of the 'Farmers Union of Hesse' in Frankfurt. Dedication to viticulture indeed. After his death in 1975 his son Erwein Graf Matuschka-Greffenclau took over the reins of Schloss Vollrads until the early 1990's when he committed suicide in his beloved vineyard. Financial problems led to this tragedy, and the future will tell whether the tradition can be carried on by another member of the Matsuchka-Greiffenclau family.

The Matuschka-Greiffenclau/Schloss Vollrads history is given prominence in the book 'The Paragon of Wines and Spirits' edited by Mark Russel (1973).

Albucasis, Arnoldo de Vilanova and Ortholaus

The distillation of alcohol was practiced by the Arabs as early as 900 A.D. but the first distillation of wine was reported by the Cordoba (Spain) Doctor Albucasis in the 12th century. Abucasis gave a detailed description of the equipment he used.

Another Spanish Doctor, Arnoldo de Vilanova (1240 - 1311) applied more scientific principles to the art of distillation and these spirits were most likely used for medicinal purposes and to fortify wines. It was not until 1358 that we had confirmation from Ortholaus, in his 'Pratica Alchimica', that distillates were properly rectified so that they could be consumed safely. With the poisonous methanol removed, this then marked the beginning of the appreciation of distilled wine i.e. brandy as we know it today.

The Jesuits

The Jesuit monks brought European vine seeds to Baja California in 1590 and grafted cuttings onto indigenous rootstocks to grow grapes for their communion wine because transporting wine from Mexico, where they have grown grapes for that purpose since 1520, was too cumbersome.

Dom Perignon

As a young man of nineteen, Dom Perignon renounced the worldly life, and just ten years later, in 1668, he was appointed Cellarer of the Benedictine Abbey of Hautvilliers, Epernay, France.

He made better wines than any other wine maker at the time, his secret being the blending of the right grapes from the best vineyards. He is reported to have had the best of all palates and he put it to good use. He was not just a good winemaker but also supervised the management of the vineyards and thus decided when the grapes were to be harvested.

The tale that Dom Perignon invented Champagne, however, is just a tale. He produced wines in a cool climatic zone where the grapes ripen late in the season with a high level of acidity. By the time the must fermented temperatures in the cellars were too low for the yeast to convert all the grape sugar to alcohol and carbon dioxide. The bacteria that reduce the malic acid to lactic acid and carbon dioxide, being even more sensitive to temperature than yeast, could not begin the malo-lactic fermentation. Quite often then, sugar residues and malic acid were fermented in the spring when temperatures rose. The carbon dioxide released during these fermentations made the wines ´bubbly´. This phenomenon was known for centuries. Dom Perignon, however, is likely to have understood the reasons for these changes (without knowing that yeast and bacteria were involved - Louis Pasteur discovered this around 1860) and by adding more sugar in the spring more carbon dioxide gas was formed providing him with a sparkling Champagne. However, this phenomenon was short lived. The carbon dioxide evaporated in time because the bottles could not be sealed well enough to retain it. At that time Champagne could only be transported in bulk (casks) which was not practicable for sparkling Champagne.

The story goes that two monks from Portugal visited the Abbey carrying, among other provisions, bottles of Portuguese wine sealed with stoppers from the cork oak that grew in Portugal. Dom Perignon soon realised the potential of such a perfect closure and perfected the technique of bottle fermentation, no doubt with lots of bottles bursting if too much sugar was added. Later better bottles were produced and sugar additions standardised.

Dom Perignon died in 1715 and just ten years later the King passed a decree that allowed Champagne to be shipped in ´osier baskets´ (hampers) holding 50 or 100 bottles. Soon sparkling Champagne became the favourite wine at the Courts of Paris, London and later also in Russia; especially among the ladies. André Simon very charmingly relates several stories of Society Ladies imbibing too much Champagne and the events at that time generally in his book ´The History of Champagne´, (1962).

Nicolas Ruinart

Ruinart Pére et Fils are the oldest Champagne shippers. Dom Thierry Ruinart, a Benedictine monk of Saint-Germain-des-Prés, a frequent visitor to Haut Villiers and an acquaintance of Dom Perignon, owned a vineyard at Reims. The wine was sold in bulk by his nephew Nicolas Ruinart, a cloth merchant of Epernay, to his customers.

In 1728 Luis XV gave the city of Reims permission to transport Champagne wine in bottles. Nicolas Ruinart is on record in 1729, of being the first to sell bottled Champagne i.e. to make use of this decree. Eventually his wine business was so successful, that his son Claude gave up the textile trade and concentrated on the making and selling of Champagne.

Ruinart Pére et Fils has grown to one of the largest Champagne houses and are the owners of many of the historic chalk cellars (formerly Roman chalk pits and now classified as a historical monument) of Reims. The company is now part of 'Moét et Chandon'.

Pedro Domecq

Don Pedro Domecq was the architect of the famous Sherry business although the foundation was laid by an Irishman, Patrick Murphy, a bachelor who left his bodega to his friend Juan Hauri when he died in 1762. Upon his death in 1794 Juan Hauri in turn left the business to his five nephews one of which was Pedro Domecq, the son of Hauri´s sister Doña Maria Lembey, who had married a Domecq. The Domecq family had their roots in France.

Juan Carlos Hauri, a cousin of Pedro Domecq Labey, was in charge of the business in Jerez while Pedro Domecq was working with their London agents Gordon, Murphy & Co. to gain business experience in England which was their biggest market.

Juan Carlos, being proud of his French ancestry, used his family connection to secure the provisions for the Emperor Napolean Bonaparte's army during his occupation of Jerez (1810 - 1812). He had the power to confiscate all the army's needs and this made him extremely unpopular to the point of being ruined and jailed.

Don Pedro Domecq now began to direct the affairs of the business, and against all the odds, managed to expand sales to England via the new agents Ruskins, Telford & Domecq. Later Don Pedro, although in overall charge, spent most of his time in Paris and London leaving the day to day running of the business to Juan Sanches who became a famous (and rich) roving winemaker. Bodegas Domecq became prosperous and famous to this day.

This fascinating story is very well related in much more detail by Julian Jeffs in his book ´Sherry´ (1961) in the Faber series of wine books.

Claude Moét

Moét et Chandon, the company that was founded by Claude Moét in 1743, has the distinction of being in every sense of the word the biggest of the Champagne houses. The business has grown to more than a thousand acres of vineyards, the cellars are 16 miles long with about 80 million bottles and the company sell annually an excess of 18 million bottles of top quality Champagne.

The management of the business passed from Claud Moét to his son Nicolas-Claude Moét, then to his son Jean-Rémy Moét (who was a friend of the emperor Napoleon). Then Victor Moét and son-in-law Pierre Gabriel Chandon came and the name was changed to Moét et Chandon.

In 1930 the company bought the Dom Perignon brand name and in 1936 their most prestigious cuveé 'Dom Perignon' was launched. This was the idea of their then UK representative André L. Simon who became a legend in his own right as wine writer and connoisseur of fine wines and food.

Fra Junipero Serra

This Franciscan missionary from Mallorca, Spain, became very active in early California. He founded several missions but from the point of view of wine making the most interesting is the ´Mission San Gabriel´ which Fra Junipero founded in 1771.

There, he built the mission winery which is the oldest existing winery in North America. Fra Junipero made wine from Vitis vinifera vines long before The Christian Brothers (1830), Jean Luis Vignes (1830), Mariano Vallejo (1836) and Agoston Haraszhy (1856). The latter is often referred to as the ´father of California viticulture´.

From the Mission vine (the researcher George Pettit, of the University of California, has identified it as the red Vinifera variety known in southern Europe as ´Monica´, the friars made a dry white altar wine and a sweet dessert wine called ´Angelica´. Angelica is a fortified wine produced in a similar fashion to Port wine, with 20% alcohol. It is made to this day.

The Franciscans were the only noteworthy wine growers until the secularization of the religious houses in 1834-35. Desmond Seward describes fully the developments that led to the Franciscan monks success and the secularization of the religious houses in California in his book ´Monks and Wine´(1979).

Arthur Phillip

Captain Arthur Phillip R.N. disembarked in Australia with his cargo of convicts (free men and vines). By 1788, as Governor of Australia, he had planted a three hectar vineyard on the grounds of Government House near Parramatta which was probably the first Australian vineyard.

William Speechley

William Speechley was the gardner of the Duke of Portland at Welbeck, Nottinghamshire, who is on record of having deliberately cross-pollinated vines to produce new varieties.

He spent seven years collecting over a hundred vine varieties and in 1790 he published his practical and well illustrated book 'A Treatise on the cultivation of the Vine' with the subtitle 'Propagation, Cultivation and Training'. The book was so popular that two further editions were printed in 1805 and 1821.

Philip Schaffer

By 1791 the German emigrant Philip Schaffer had planted his one acre vineyard on the banks of the Parramatta river, New South Wales, which is recognised as the first private, commercial vineyard of Australia.

Nicole-Barbe Ponsardin

Phillipe Cliquot was a banker and textile merchant who set up a Champagne business in 1772 in Reims with his wife's dowry of vineyards in Bouzy and Verzenay. He did not make commercial quantities of wine. His son François was more interested in wine and when he married Nicole-Barbe Ponsardin in 1799, the daughter of a wealthy citizen of Reims, he sold the bank and concentrated on the making of Champagne. Both François and his father Phillipe died early.

Instead of giving up the business Nicole-Barbe, at the age of only 27, took on the challenge and established the house of Veuve Cliquot-Ponsardin & Co. Success came with the appointment of M. Bohne as sales representative. Practically all the Champagne was sold to Russia.

What made Nicole-Barbe a pioneer for the entire Champagne industry was her invention, together with her young German manager Edouard Merlé, the shaking and twisting of bottles to deposit the yeast after the bottle fermentation to obtain a clear Champagne (the forerunner of the pupitre table for the remuage). This remuage is still practiced today but for large Champagne producers it has been partly mechanised.

Veuve Cliquot-Ponsardin is to this day one of the leading Champagne houses with descendants of Edouard Werlé still holding responsible positions in its management.

1800 A.D. - 1900 A.D.

This period heralded the beginning of great technological advances in wine making.

Jean-Antoine Chaptal introduced the practice of adding sugar to French must so as to increase the alcohol content of wine, especially in off vintages, when weather conditions were unfavourable.

More important, however, was the discovery by Louis Pasteur that yeasts are responsible for the fermentation that turns sugar into alcohol, lactic bacteria reduce high acid levels by converting malic acid to the milder lactic acid and carbon dioxide and acetobacter, which convert alcohol to vinegar, given the right conditions. This knowledge revolutionised wine making procedures, and when it was finally understood by the wine makers, wine quality improved considerably.

Also at this time our wine grape 'Vitis vinifera sativa' continued its conquest of the new world. European emigrants planted vines in the American continent, Australia and New Zealand.

It must have been an exciting time for all wine pioneers, although it was connected with hard work and frequent setbacks because in the mid 1880s vine diseases like oidium (powdery mildew), peronospera (downy mildew) and the dreaded phylloxera, exported from America, destroyed Europe's vineyards and European vines planted in the new world. It was also the time of the foundation of many now famous wine estates world wide.

Jean-Antoine Chaptal (Compte de Chanteloup)

Jean Chaptal was a distinguished chemist and the first Professor of chemistry at the University of Montpellier. From 1800 - 1805 he was Ministre de l'Interieur (Home Secretary) when he gave instructions to the vignerons to add cane sugar to unfermented must at vintage time to raise the potential alcohol content. This practice has become known as ´chaptalisation´ and is widespread in the northern wine regions from Bordeaux (in some years) to Burgundy, Loire, Champagne, Germany etc.

The addition of sugar provides more alcohol than nature has provided in poor vintages and allows wine makers to produce drinkable wines even in off years. During the fermentation sugar is converted to alcohol, carbon dioxide, glycerol, higher alcohols etc. and thus the quality is improved, quite apart from increasing the alcohol content. The effect is reversed if too much sugar is added; it produces unbalanced wines. For this reason strict controls limit sugar additions from year to year.

Chaptal's decree gave, above all, Champagne makers the chance to introduce a secondary fermentation after the wine has been bottled. The resultant carbon dioxide is the essential ingredient of Champagne.

´Chaptalisation´ was not universally popular. Chaptal's compatriote Parmentier preferred the use of grape juice concentrate (sirop de raisons), and in 1812 he published his ´Apercus des résultats obtenus de la fabrication des sirops et conserves de raisins dans le cours des années 1810 et 1811´.

Since perfecting the reverse-osmosis process in the late 1980´s, which permits the extraction of 10 - 20% water from low quality grape must, the additions of sugar and grape juice concentrates have become less important.

Andreas Jordan and Dr. H. C. Friedrich von Bassermann (Bassermann-Jordan)

Andreas Jordan, a member of a family who owned vineyards in the Rheinpfalz, Germany, since 1718, bought the 'Ketschauer Hof' (Deidesheim) in 1816 which has a history of wine making dating back to 1250. Andreas set about to modernise the vineyards and is considered the founder of German quality viticulture.
There being no male descendents his son-in-law continued the tradition of quality wine production.
Dr. H. C. Friedrich von Bassermann-Jordan, an internationally recognized wine historian, is also the author of the definitive work on the 'History of Viticulture' (1907-1923), an extensive study which is still the standard reference work on the subject. He was also instrumental in the establishment of the now famous 'Speyer Wine Museum'. The estate at Deidesheim now also has its own Wine Museum.

Samuel Marsden

The Anglican missionary Samuel Marsden is given credit for bringing the first vines to New Zealand. In 1819 he recorded in his journal: "We had a small spot of land cleared and broken up in which I planted about a hundred grape vines of different kinds brought from Port Jackson. New Zealand promises to be very favourable to the vine, as far as I can judge at present, from the nature of the soil and climate".

However, the honour of being the first Government viticulturist goes to Romero Bragado and the first NZ wine maker was undoubtedly James Busby.

Elizabeth Gervais

To improve the quality of her wines Mlle Gervais invented an elaborate machine that excluded air to prevent oxidation of must and wine. It included a cooling tower filled with cold water to condense alcohol and flavour vapours which are normally lost during fermentation. Her machine returned the volatile fractions to the young wine.

Her brother Jean wrote about this interesting machine in a report dated 1820 and Louis XVIII granted her a patent for it. From our present perspective this seems to have been a good idea coming close to a temperature controlled fermentation, but it had no followers at the time.

James Busby

James Busby, born in Scotland, is considered the father of Australian viticulture.

He came to Australia in 1824 with his father, a civil engineer, who was assigned to develop a water system for the city of Sydney. As soon as he learned that he would be emigrating to Australia James Busby visited the vineyards of France to learn all he could about the planting of vines and wine making. In his first book ´A Treatese on the cultivation of the Vine and the Art of Making Wines´, published in 1825, he passed on the information he had gathered.

He brought cuttings to Australia and in 1828 he planted the first three acre vineyard in the Hunter Valley which he called 'Kirkton' after his birthplace in Scotland. Together with George Wynn he pioneered the marketing of Australian wines although Wynn's first vineyard in the Hunter Valley was abandoned during the rural depression of the 1840s.

James Busby made several excursions to European vineyards and shipped cuttings of many grape varieties and reported progress in several more books. Later, disenchanted with the support and recognition he received in Australia, he left for New Zealand where, in 1833, he again planted a vineyard at Waitangi and pioneered NZ wine making. The wines Busby made found favour with the Imperial troops and in 1840 by a visiting French explorer Dumont d'Urville.

Jean Luis Vignes/Don Luis Aliso

Jean Luis Vignes, a cooper from. Cadillac, France, came to El Pueblo de Nuestro Señora la Reina de Los Angeles de Porciuncula (today's Los Angeles) around 1830. He planted the local Mission vines but soon found that they did not produce wines of a quality he was used to from home and imported vine cuttings from France. His wines and brandies became so popular that he could sell them to many parts of California. To build up his business even further he invited two of his nephews to come from France to help him.

Although the Jesuits and the Franciscan Fra Junipero Serra (the famous Franciscan monk who built the now oldest north American winery at the 'San Gabrial Mission' which was founded in 1771) made wine long before Vignes.

Vignes, however, was the first winemaker and distiller in California to make a commercial success with wines from European vines.

Vignes won wide acclaim, became very rich, changed his name to Don Luis Aliso and was soon only known as ´Don Luis´.

Juan Sanchez

Juan Sanches, the son of a well to do Santander family came to Jerez (Spain) around 1830, where he began making Sherry from grapes grown in his own vineyards.

He became an extraordinarily good winemaker with contracts to make and blend wine for a number of Jerez bodega owners, including the infamous Juan Carlos Hauri, later for Don Pedro Domecq and others. For Duff Gordon & Co. he is reported to have prepared a blend of Sherry that was of such excellent quality that sales had to be discontinued because the base wines reached such high prices and the blend could not be sold profitably.

Sanches was probably the first roving winemaker; although our modern, international wine makers, are engaged on several continents whereas he was confined to Jerez.

Sanches died in 1861 a wealthy man.

Joseph James Forrester (Baron de Forrester)

The adulteration of Portuguese wine with alcohol, elderberry wine and inferior wines from other regions had taken on unacceptable proportions when Joseph James

Forrester arrived in Oporto in 1831 to work for is uncle. At that time table (unfortified) wines from the Douro were very popular in England, and Forrester became rightly concerned what these practices might do to the reputation of the port wine trade and he set about to write articles to stop these ´improvements´. Needless to say this did not make him very popular with some of his less scrupelous contemporaries. However, he persisted and succeeded as far as the addition of elderberry and other wines were concerned, but the additions of grape brandy was legalised; and this is how Port, the fortified wine as we now know it, has evolved.

Apart from being successful wine makers - Forresters are still well known Port producers - Baron de Forrester was also a talented painter, the first cartographer of the Duoro River district and a prolific writer.

Manuel Maria Gonzalez Angel

After his marriage in 1833, to the daughter of the richest man in Cadiz, Don Manuel moved to Jerez where he had bought a small bodega with his then meager savings in the hope that he could sell wines to support his new wife. With the capital of a Señor Aguera he set up his business in 1835 and soon began exporting Sherry to England.

The first year's shipments amounted to no more than 10 butts (1 butt = 490 l) by 1839, now from his new bodega, it was 819 butts. Señor Aguera lost his nerve and withdrew his capital. His new partner, Juan Dubose became actively involved in selling wines as far a field as Germany and Russia so that by 1873 sales reached 10,400 butts.

The business in England was further developed by their English agent, Robert Blake Byass, who later became a partner, hence the name Gonzalez Byass & Co. The company became famous throughout the world with their dry fino Sherry 'Tio Pepe' (uncle Joe). Gonzalez Byass export a full range of top quality Sherries and Brandy.

Mariano (General) Vallejo

General Vallejo was the last Mexican military commandant of Sonoma, California, and founder of the town of Sonoma. He revived viticulture at the 'Sonoma Mission' around 1836 and in 1851, upon his retirement, he established his own vineyard at Lachryma Montis in Sonoma County. His venture attracted other growers to the area and in 1856 the famous Agoston Haraszthy became his neighbour and friend.

Ephram Bull

The native American vine variety 'Vitis labrusca' (labrusca = wild vine), is largely immune to the diseases and pests prevailing in the US (and now Europe), but the new settlers were not impressed with the quality of the wines that were produced from these grapes.

The Vitis vinifera, brought by them from Europe, could not withstand the native pests phylloxera, peronospera, oidium etc. despite the efforts of such famous viticulturists as George Washington, Thomas Jefferson and Benjamin Franklin to find remedies. New varieties emerged, but even the wines from 'Catawba' or 'Isabella' did not satisfy the wine consumer.

In 1849 Ephram Bull of Concord, Massachusetts introduced a new variety (probably a cross of two Labruscas) which he named 'Concord'. This is now the most widely planted variety in the eastern US despite the fact that the 'foxy' characteristics are still evident. They are, however, accepted in sweet (dessert) wines.

Agoston Haraszthy

Agoston Haraszthy, a Hungarian nobleman, fled from his homeland and immigrated with his family to the United States in 1840. In 1849 he came to San Diego, California, where he became sheriff and town marshall, and in 1852 he was elected to the State Assembly and moved to San Francisco.

In 1856 he purchased the 'Buena Vista Ranch' in Sonoma County and there he became active in commercial wine making. He planted nearly 140 acres, mainly with Mission vines. Not being too happy with the quality of the wines, he travelled through European vineyards and subsequently imported some 100.000 vines of some 300 varieties to replant his vineyards. It is thought that the successful Zinfandel was one of the varieties he imported. To finance the early years of this venture he sold vines from his Buena Vista nursery and thus his name is associated with the birth of modern viticulture in California and he is often referred to as the 'father of California viticulture', although it was known that Fra Junipero Serra already made wine from the Vitis vinifera (known as the 'Mission grape') in 1771 and Jean Luis Vignes made large quantities of wine around 1830 from imported French Vinifera varieties.

Haraszthy wrote a number of books; the most interesting is entitled 'Grape culture, wines and wine-making' (1862).

He founded the ´Buena Vista Viticultural Society´ at Sonoma which at that time made Sonoma the foremost viticultural centre of California.

Sadly, Haraszthy was alleged to have mismanaged the Buena Vista Ventures and was forced to leave in 1869, disappearing without ever being seen again.

Thomas Hardy

The SS British Empire brought Thomas Hardy, a twenty year old farmer from Devon, to Adelaide in 1850. After jobbing as a butcher in the Victoria gold fields he returned to Adelaide with his savings and bought in 1853 a property called Bankside and planted 16 acres of vines. He made the first wine a few years later.

He and his wife Joanna worked hard and by 1863 they had doubled the size of the vineyard. In 1876 he acquired the Tintara vineyard from Dr. Alexander Kelly, another pioneer of Australian viticulture. Kelly published his first book ´The Vine in Australia´ in 1861. He was not a good businessman, but Harry's enterprise went from strength to strength.

To this day Thomas Hardy & Sons Pty Ltd. is one of Australia's largest and respected wine companies. Thomas Hardy was a President of the ´Vigneron's Association´ and held other important posts. He is the only Australian winemaker who was honoured by the people of McLaren Vale. They erected a memorial in the town square.

Don Camilo Hurtado de Amézaga de Riscal, Marqués de Riscal

The Marqués de Riscal saw the potential for the wines of Rioja, Spain, when they were in great demand, following the devastation of French grape harvests by the powdery mildew (oidium) which had been imported from North America in the 1840s.

In 1850 Don Camilo founded his bodega, now known as Heredos del Marqués de Riscal S.A. in Elciego, in the heart of the Rioja country, to meet the needs of the French wine merchants.

A few years after oidium the dreaded aphid phylloxera came to Bordeaux and caused even greater damage to French vineyards. The popularity of Rioja wines thus increased further. French vignerons came to Rioja to add their skills to make Bordeaux style wines and one of these experts was M. Jean Pineaux. However, his services were not universally accepted, but the Marqués de Riscal decided to engage him and in 1860 had a new bodega built to his design. The bodega had all the features that were in vouge in Bordeaux at the time with the ´chai de conservation´, the ´chai de vinification´ and the ´atelier de tonnellerie´ the latter with ample capacity for oak casks (barriques) to mature the wines.

The Riscal bodega is the oldest in Rioja although modernised to handle the grapes from 300 hectares of the Elciego vineyards, mostly planted with Tempranillo, also some Cabernet Sauvignon and Viura vines.

One of the unique features at the bodega is the world's largest vinotheques known as the ´catedral´ holding wines of all the vintages since 1860.

At El Ciego an ultra modern addition to the bodega, designed by the world famous architect Frank Ghery, who also built the Guggenheim museum in Bibao, was inaugurated in 1996. It is a small luxury hotel with only 14 rooms. The ultra modern design with intricate passages, arches and cubicles has a metal roof in rosé, silver and gold, the colours of viticulture, that gives way to breathtaking views. It is already a tourist attraction and will no doubt be enjoyed by many a wine buyer and other welcome guests.

Charles Krug

In 1858 Charles Krug, a German emigrant, was one of the first in the Napa Valley to make wines commercially in the mould of European wine makers using a small cider press.

He planted his own vineyard in 1860 and in 1861 he constructed the Krug winery where he first made wine for John Patchett. He gained a reputation as a maker of fine wines and his wines were sold throughout the United States and Europe. However, a few years later phylloxera attacked the European, ungrafted vines and wiped out about 10,000 of the estimated 17,000 acres planted at that time in the Napa Valley. Krug also suffered severe financial losses from which he never fully recovered. He died in 1892.

The Charles Krug Winery was bought, in 1943, by Cesare Mondavi, an Italian emigrant, and father of Robert Mondavi.

Louis Pasteur

This eminent French scientist, a native of the Jura district, discovered around 1860 that micro-organisms were responsible for the changes that occur during the fermentation of must and certain bacteria cause spoilage of the finished wine if precautions are not taken. He used heat to eliminate unwanted bacteria, for wine a crude way of sterilisation, which became known as ´pasteurisation´.

Pasteur's influence on wine making was profound, especially in relation to cheaper wines with a low alcohol concentration. The impact on the making of quality wines was insignificant in so far, that heating such musts and wines would have been out of the question on account of the off flavours this process introduced. However, the discovery that yeasts and bacteria were responsible for the various changes during fermentations was of utmost importance to all wine makers. Measures to control these microorganisms - other than pasteurisation - evolved so that bad (spoiled) wines are now a thing of the past.

Louis Pasteur put it this way:
"The role of the infinitely small is infinitely large."

A. Freiherr von Babo

This Austrian pioneer and researcher founded in 1860 the viticulture and wine making school at the Augustiner Chorherrenstift which later became the ´Austrian Higher Federal School and Research Centre Klosterneuburg´.

Freiherr von Babo and E. Mach published several authoritative works on viticulture and cellar technology.

Jules Guyot

Dr. Jules Guyot is best known for his vine pruning system (single or double canes for trellises); a system which was already known and used by Columella at the beginning of the first millennium A.D., but Guyot did much more.

In 1865 he published his book ´Culture of the vine and wine making´ and in 1896 an English version ´Growth of the vine and principles of winemaking´ was published in Melbourne, Australia. At that time this was the most reliable source of information for Australian wine growers and wine makers. The advice Guyot gave them was, however, for quality wines with small yields and this practice was commercially not viable because the wines produced for the consumption by colonists in the new world, as opposed to the quality wines produced in France for the rich, traditional wine drinkers of Europe, were too costly at the time.

Oscar Benno Pedro (Benno) Seppelt

Although his father, Joseph Ernst Seppelt, an emigrant from Silesia, laid the foundations for the Seppeltsfield dynasty in 1852 it was, however, Benno Seppelt who was responsible for the huge success of the then small enterprise he inherited. After the death of his father in 1866, Benno became manager of the business when just twenty one years old.

His hard work and foresight led in his lifetime to one of the largest wine companies in Australia known to this day as B. Seppelt & Sons Ltd. Benno Seppelt and his wife Sophie raised nine sons and four daughters and although Seppelt´s has become part of the Southern Brewing Company, fourth generation members of the Seppelt family are still actively involved in the business.

George Husmann

George Husmann was professor of horticulture at the University of Missouri in the 1870's when phylloxera began to destroy European vines and the dire need arose to find measures to combat this pest. He published his book 'The cultivation of the native grape and manufacture of American wines' in 1866, mainly for the German wine growers who had settled in the eastern US. His experience with native vines soon led him to suitable root stocks for European vines that provided the lasting answer to the disaster that also afflicted European vignerons. Grafting European vine cuttings onto American - phylloxera resistant rootstocks - is still the only remedy to the aphid phylloxera.

Barone Bettino Ricasoli

The Baron Bettino Ricasoli was nicknamed Barone di Ferro (Iron Baron) for good reason. In 1861 he became the second Prime Miister of the newly united Italy and for this task he had to be tough. Around 1872 the less than handsome Baron married the young and beautiful Anna Bonacorsi and soon realised that she was also desired by other men.The jealous husband simply took his youg bride to his Castello di Brolio in the Tuscan hills and kept her there forever.
The Baron was keenly interested in agriculture and without political or other destractions he later began to experiment with the cultivation of vines. At that time viticulture was a peasant occupation. The vines were trained up trees and in

mixed cultures. The wines they produced, maily from the red Sangiovese grape, were of rather poor quality and so powerful and acid that they could only be consumed diluted with water.

Baron Ricasoli cultivated the Sangiovese vines in the now traditional fashion and mixed in a proportion of the softer red Canaiolo and white muscat flavoured Malvasia to make the wine more palatable. Later he improved wine making further by introducing the ´governo system´ i.e. the must was allowed to ferment in contact with the skins for a week or ten days. After pressing he added 5 to 10% dried grapes to the young wine and thus prolonged the fermentation. This extra time encourage the malo-lactic fermentation which reduces the aggressive malic acid to the mellow lactic acid. Some of the carbon dioxide from this fermentation remained and the resulting wine was fresh, fruity and very enjoyable.

For more than a hundred and fifty years Chianti was produced by this method and became famous. In recent decades further experiments were conducted by blending Sangiovese with Cabernet Sauvignon and Merlot grapes. Opinions vary as to the wisdom of these ´improvements´ but the Chianto Classico Consorzio now permits the addition of 20% other varieties to the Sangiovese.

José Raventos

The Codorniu/Raventos families have grown grapes and made wine in Sant Sadurni de Noya, Penedes, just south of Barcelona, Spain since the 1550´s, but their success was very modest. Their fortunes changed when in 1872 José Raventos, a descendant of the Raventos who, in 1659, married the heiress of the Cordorniu family, travelled to northern Europe to learn more about wine making. In the Champagne region he learned the art of Champagne making. With that information and some useful equipment he came home to Catalonia where he made the first Spanish ´methode champenoise´ sparkling wine. The principle difference between Cava, as Spanish sparkling wines are called because the Champagne makers have secured the right to the name Champagne for themselves, are the grape varieties. The white grapes Parrelada, Macabeo and Xarel-lo are to this day the mainstay of Cava production whereas the Champenoise use the white Chardonnay and the red Pinot Noir and Pinot Meunier.

Raventos´ efforts were successful indeed and laid the foundation for Codorniu, today´s largest sparkling wine producer in the world. Their production now runs to some 200 million bottles per annum. The quality of most of the Cavas, although lighter in character than Champagne, is excellent and the prices are affordable. Today Codorniu and its main competitor Freixenet, which was founded in 1887, each produce more than 25% of the total Cava production

Eugene Hilgard

Professor Eugene Hilgard laid the foundations for scientific viticulture when, in 1880, the ´Agricultural Experiment Station´ was established in California. He pointed out that in parts of California the climate could be too benign for viticulture and with his assistant, later to be his successor, Professor Bioletti, divided the wine growing regions by climate.

A. J. Winkler developed, at the University of California in Davis, this idea further and in 1936 he published a scale of ´degree days´ which measures the length of time the thermometer remains over 50° F between 1st April and 31st

October. If the mean temperature over five days was 70°F, the summation of heat would be (70-50= 20) x 5 = 100 degree days.

The regions are thus:
I   2500   degree days or less
II   2501 to 3000 "   "
III 3001 to 3500 "   "
IV   3501 to 4000 "   "
V   More than 4000 degree days.

Using this scale, also in other regions, wine growers can now choose the vine variety that best suits their climates. For example Chardonnay makes the best wines in region I (cool), Cabernet Sauvignon in region II or III (moderately warm) Sauvignon Blanc and Zinfandel in region IV or V (warm).

H.Müller (Thurgau)

In 1882 Dr. Dr. Hermann. Müller, a native of the Swiss Canton of Thurgau, was assistant researcher at the ´Viticultural Research Institute´ Geisenheim (Germany), where he experimented with vine crossings.

In 1891 he took up a post at the Swiss research institute Wädenswil. He took the seedlings with him to continue his work there. His assistant, Dr. H. Schellenberg, observed that one of the vines, then thought to be a cross between Riesling and Silvaner (actually Riesling x Madeleine Royal) had promising characteristics, including vigorous growth, early ripening, good fruit and - even after early spring frost damage-the vines yielded crops because the auxiliary buds that replaced frost affected shoots bore reasonable quantities of fruit in the same season. It was

Schellenberg who discovered the potential of this new vine, but it was named after its breeder Müller-Thurgau.

Melchor de Concha y Toro

Although it was Don Ramon Subercaseaux Mercado who bought the first estates for the family on the outskirts of Santiago de Chile with the money he made in his silver mines, irrigated the arid land and even planted the first French vines, credit must go to Don Melchor de Concha y Toro, the Marques de Casa de Concha and his wife Dona Emiliana, doughter of Don Ramon for being the first to produce commercial quantities of European style wines in Chile. They had the vision and courage in 1883 to plant extensive vineyards with new imports of French vines and, with the help of the French Expert M. de Labouchere made classic quality wines.

The vineyards of Concha y Toro now extent to some 4,500 hectares in the principle wine regions of Chile i.e. Maipo, Maule, Rapel, Colchagua, Curico and Casablanca. The vine varieties are Cabernet Sauvignon, Merlot, Malbec, Semillon, Riesling, Sauvignon Blanc, Chardonnay, Gewuerztraminer and some Chenin Blanc. The wines they produce are of excellent quality not only because of favourable climatic conditions but also because the vines can mature to 50 or 100 years due to the fact that they are not grafted on American rootstocks. Phylloxera never reached Chilean vineyards.

Concha y Toro are the largest producers of quality wines in Chile and the most successful exporters.

Charles William Henry Kohler

A former prospector in the Johannesburg gold rush (1890) Charles Kohler, came to farming when he became too ill for gold mining. He bought a 140 acre farm on the Berg River and planted vines. This was the worst possible time for such a venture, because phylloxera ravished the vines and wine prices dropped to below production cost. However, Charles Kohler was a resourceful man, and by founding the Ko-operatieve Wijnbouwers Vereniging (KWV), he and many of his farmer/vigneron friends survived; and to this day the KWV is one of the leading wine producers of South Africa.

Theobald Friedrich Seitz

During his time as a wine merchant Theo Seitz, like most of his compatriots, met problems with unstable wines and suffered financial losses through secondary fermentation, bacterial spoilage etc. Being a man of resolve he invented the first wine
filter and in 1891 he founded the Seitz-Filter Werke in Bad Kreuznach, Germany. He discovered that asbestos, mixed with cellulose fibres, provided an excellent filter media. He also established one of the first commercial wine research laboratories.
In 1913 he appointed Dr. Friedrich Schmitthenner as head of of his laboratory. In 1916 Schmitthenner invented the first filter capable of sterilising, mechanically, wine, water etc. To sterilize liquids was a fundamental invention and Seitz designed new filters with greater capacity. By pressing the asbestos (later replaced partly with diatomaceous earth) and cellulose fibres into compact filter sheets brought greater reliability and efficiency.

Wine making and wine marketing was thus revolutionised and to this day Seitz-Werke are leaders in the design and manufacture of filters and bottling machines.

Romeo Bragato

The Dalmation born Romeo Bragato, a graduate of the 'Italian Royal School of Viticulture and Oenology' at Corregliano came to New Zealand by invitation of the government in 1895 to investigate the possibilities for viticulture and wine making in their country and thus became the first official viticulturist of the then British colony. James Busby, however, was the first to make NZ wine from grapes grown in his small vineyard planted at Waitangi in 1836. The wines Busby made found favour with the Imperial troops and, in 1840, by the visiting French explorer Dumont d'Urville.

Bragato's report was most favourable for widespread viticulture, but early setbacks due to phylloxera, oidium, the prohibitionists and uninformed politicians, the New Zealand wine industry was slow to grow. In 1901 Bragato accepted the newly created post of Government viticulturist with the express brief to deal with phylloxera. He developed the government station at Te Kauwhata and grafted vines onto American, phylloxera resistant, rootstocks and replanted the vineyard that was first established there in 1897.

Another government vineyard was planted in 1903 at Arataki in Hawkes Bay. At Te Kauwhata, Bragato set up an experimental winery where he made good wine from Vitis vinifera grape varieties. However, Bragato's vision of a thriving NZ wine industry was not shared by all department heads. His efforts were curtailed and in 1909 he left disillusioned for Canada where eventually he committed suicide.

Despite this unfortunate turn of events, Bragato´s heritage bore fruit in the end. New Zealand wines, especially the white wines Sauvignon Blanc and Chardonnay, are now rated among the best in the world.

Francis Lawrence Berry, Charles Walter Berry and Hugh Rudd.

Number ´Three Saint James´s Street´, London, is probably the most famous of all wine merchants addresses. Since the Jacobite Rebellion, it housed a grocery store, and the Scales to which members of the High Society came to be weighed. From 1765 progress in gains or losses of their weight were duly recorded for posterity, but never disclosed to outsiders during the lifetime of those weighed.

Before changing to wine sales exclusively in 1896 Berry Brothers and Co. also traded in coffee, tea and other groceries. Fame as wine merchants, and even more prosperity, were created by Henry Berry, and later by the second cousins Francis Lawrence Berry and Charles Walter Berry. In 1920 Major Hugh R. Rudd became a partner and in 1945 the firm was renamed to Berry Brothers and Rudd Ltd. Royalty and the upper classes were, and are, among their customers, simply because they are sold exceptionally good quality wines and brandies. Later their own brand of whisky, ´Cutty Sark´, became very popular, especially in the US. The prestige of the firm is unparalleled.

H. Warner Allen published in his book ´Number Three St. James´s Street - A history of Berry Brother's the Wine Merchants´ (1950), an amusing tale:

"A certain noble customer had owed the firm an increasing sum of money for a very long time, and Henry Berry, after much hesitation, finally decided that the time had come when a definitive step should be taken to recover the debt. A firm but exceedingly courteous letter was composed and sent off to the noble Lord, who replied by return of post that he had received Mr.Berry´s letter and was so distressed by its contents that the only remedy which could restore him to his usual health would be a dozen bottles of Mr. Berry's finest Brandy. This letter was doubtless received with great amusement and surprise, only equaled by the astonishment of the customer when a dozen bottles were delivered the following day. It is pleasant to be able to record that, after this unexpected action by both parties; the account was promptly settled."

It shows the character and attitude of Henry Berry, and the debt collectors of our time could take a leaf out of that book.

Francis Berry, a Gentleman in every sense of the word, represented the firms' interests abroad, in particular the USA. Charles Walter Berry travelled widely to procure the best wines that were available. He described one of his excursions through European vineyards in his book ´In Search of Wine´(1935). The directors entertained lavishly at Number Three and in his amusing book ´Viniana´ (1934) Charles Walter Berry gave vivid accounts of the dinners at which fabulous wines were served.

Hugh Rudd, who spoke fluent German, came to the partnership just in time to select the best wines from the greatest German vintage ever, the 1921. It was a difficult vintage insofar as the growers had no experience with such an abundance of grape sugar and concentrated extracts. Many wines started a secondary fermentation after bottling but the Ausleses and Beerenausleses presented no such difficulties and were in great demand, also in England. In his book ´Hocks and Moselles´ (1935) Hugh R. Rudd takes the reader through all the German wine regions with expert commentary about the wines and the people who made them.

M. Chrétien Oberlin

The Agronomic Station at Rouffach (Alsace) needed a new home, and with the wine industry in Alsace having been devastated by phylloxera and other diseases the city of Colmar became interested and began to support the wine growers in their efforts to replant vineyards with suitable vines. For 30 years M. Oberlin had collected vines to find the answer to phylloxera.

The government approached him to take on the task formally, and in 1897 the ´Oberlin Wine Institute Colmar´ was established. Oberlin's seedlings were transferred, and research continued. Among the cuttings was the now famous Gewürztraminer which, with Riesling, became the mainstay of the outstanding wines of Alsace. Oberlin recommended that vineyards are replanted with vines grafted on the phylloxera resistant rootstock Riparia x Rupestris 3309.

1900 - 1950

Wine making made enormous progress in this period. Excellent vintages such as 1900, 1921, 1928 and 1949, were harvested and technology had advanced sufficiently to keep the wines sound and stable, so that they could mature to realize their full potential. These superb vintages were not expected by many experts who had predicted a downturn in quality from the now grafted vines. Pre-phylloxera vines were considered superior.

Idealism and individualism were still features that left their mark on the wines that were made. Wine drinking was, by and large, the privilege of the middle and upper classes and they chose their wines with care. Prices were kept reasonable by the fact that consumption was limited. There was thus a healthy, competitive environment with value for money being offered. Wine merchants had personal contacts to their suppliers and their clientele. This close relationship between producer, merchant and wine consumer led to the establishment of many first class estates and wine merchandising houses of which some of the best have survived to this day.

Julius Wegeler

The most famous German vineyard is undoubtedly the 'Bernkasteler Doktor', a 3.3 hectar vineyard on the edge of Bernkastel. In 1900 Julius Wegeler bought a part of the vineyard (the other part owners are Thanisch and Lautenberg) to ensure supplies of this prestigious wine, and paid the record sum of 100 gold marks per vine.

The Wegeler family were wine growers since 1794 and extended their wine estates to some 100 hectares of the best vineyards on the Moselle (Bernkastel, Graach), the Rheingau (Oestrich) and the Rheinpfalz (Deidesheim).

The trade knows the Wegeler enterprises better for their marketing company ´Deinhard of Kobenz´, one of Germany's oldest sparkling wine producers. Wegeler/Deinhard are, by any standard, among Germany's most respected wine houses.

Frédéric Emile Hugel

The Hugel Family has made wine in Alsace since 1639, when Hans Ulrich Hugel was made a freeman of Riquewihr and presided over the ´Wine Growers Guild´.

The wine estate, as we now know it today, however, was founded in 1902 by Frédéric Emile Hugel, who left the old family property and established himself at new premises in the centre of Riquewihr, which to this day is the heart of the Alsace wine region.

After the ravages of phylloxera, oidium, peronospera and later world war I, pioneers like Frederic Emile Hugel replanted the vineyards with classical vine varieties, mainly Riesling and Gewuerztraminer, and made wines of a quality that made history. His son Jean enhanced the reputation of Hugel and the wines of Alsace generally. Jean's sons Georges, Jean and André still make some of the finest wines from the famous grape varieties Riesling and Gewürztraminer, which are grown in Alsace´ best vineyards sites, namely Riquewihr´s 'Sporon' and 'Schoenenberg', which are largely owned by the Hugel family.

Assid Abraham Corban

The Lebanese born A. A. Corban came to New Zealand via Australia in 1892. In 1902 he bought a four hectar plot of land and progressively established his vineyard at Henderson (with Chasselas, Hermitage and Cabernet Sauvignon), with the aim of making quality wine. He succeeded - later with the help of his two sons Wadier and Khaled - to make theirs the most successful wine business that survived even the Prohibition. Corban's is the oldest NZ winery, all be it now widely expanded and owned by Rothmans because the present generation, Joe and Alex Corban, found it impossible to raise sufficient capital to finance the necessary investments for expansion to the present, viable, business.

Rudolf Jordan Jr.

This California winemaker has experimented successfully with cold fermentations and yeast cultures in his winery at Castle Rock, Napa Valley, which is now the site of the famous Christian Brothers Noviate ´Mont La Salle´ vineyard. His new style California wines where light, dry and fruity.

Rudolf Jordan Jr. reported details of the techniques he employed in his book ´A Manual for Progressive Winemakers in California´ (1911), probably the earliest record referring to cold fermentation with selected yeast cultures.

Friedrich Schmitthenner

Wines very frequently suffered spoilage in the past because yeast or bacteria became active during storage given the right temperature.

Residual sugars would be fermented, malic acid reduced to lactic acid in the so called ´malo-lactic fermentation´ and alcohol converted to vinegar etc. To avoid these problems Port and Sherry, for example, were fortified to inhibit bacteria with 16% alcohol and yeast with about 22%. Table wines with 10 to 12 % alcohol are not protected, especially if unfermented sugars are present.

Help came in 1916 when Dr. Schmitthenner, chief chemist of the Seitz-Werke, Bad Kreuznach, Germany, developed a filter using cellulose and asbestos fibers (the health hazards of asbestos were not known at that time and asbestos was later replaced by other fibers and diatomatious earth) to form filter beds so fine as to retain micro-organisms. From these beginnings the famous ´EK´ (EntKeimung) filter sheet for pressure filters was developed. This revolutionised the wine industry because now, low strength wines could be bottled with residual sugar, sterile bottling making it possible. Even red wines, which are sold young, need sterile filtration to avoid the malo-lactic fermentation if the wine is not given time before being bottled.

Henri Gouge

In the early 20th century, the blending of wines from various regions was still common practice in France, and to protect their good reputations, and the identity of their wines, people like the Marquis d´ Angerville from Volnay (then President of l´Union Géneral de Syndicats pour la Défence des Producteurs de Grands Vins de Bourgogne) and Henri Gouge (succeeding Angerville as President) fought many a legal battle against fraudulent blending and fraudulent descriptions of wines sold under the good name of 'Bourgogne'. This fight cost them dearly in so far, that the merchant closed ranks against them and no longer bought their wines.

Henri Gauge started to market his own wine which was grown in the prestigious vineyards in the commune of 'Nuit St. George'. He was always experimenting to improve his cepage, mainly Pinot Noir and Chardonnay, and in doing so, he discovered, around 1934, a clone of Pinot Noir bearing white grapes. Cuttings of this vine were planted and the offshoots also produced white grapes.

Henri Gouge died in 1967, but his sons Michel and Henri, to this day, make this unique white Pinot Noir. Domaine Henri Gouges are famed for their white and red wines made from the vines Henri Sr. had so carefully selected. Their red Pinot Noir bear very small crops but outstanding wines and other use cuttings for their own vineyards.

Henri Woltner

Although his father bought the now famous Chateau La Mission Haut Brion in 1918 it was Henri Waltner who brought about the changes that made the wines famous when he became the manager in 1921. Together with his brother, Fernand, he restructured the vineyards to yield better quality grapes. The harvest was started when the grapes were just ripe and not overripe - when the grape flavours were at their peak of development.

Later the innovative Henri introduced new technological wine making methods, hitherto unheard of in Bordeaux, and frequently out-did some of his more famous neighbours. His wines were rated on equal, and sometimes superior, terms than the so called first growth of Bordeaux. Whereas previously the wines were fermented in large vats or casks, which often led to overheating during the fermentation and produced off flavours; Woltner introduced glass lined steel tanks and a cooling system to keep the fermentation temperature below 28° C. The wines gained enormously from more and cleaner flavours.

In 1928 the Woltner brothers bought 'Chateau Laville-Haut-Brion', where they made white wines only and gained the reputation for making the best traditional Graves that was at its best when 8 to 10 years old.

Baron Philippe de Rothschild

As a young man of 20, Baron Philippe de Rothschild was sent to Bordeaux in 1922 by his father Baron Henri to take charge of the then, in his own words: "old forgotten farm" of Chateau Mouton.

The Chateau made some of the finest wines of Bordeaux with only the wines of Ch. Lafite, Ch. Margaux, Ch.Latour and Ch. Haut-Brion considered to be better. The 1855 classification, which was part of the 'Exposition Universelle de Paris', organised by Napoleon III, was based on the prices paid to the best Bordeaux wines over the preceding hundred years rather than the judgement of the commission members. Ch.Mouton did well to come fifth in the rating (or first in the second growth category), bearing in mind that there was no organised management, and presumably, no proper marketing structure at the Chateau which would have seen to better prices being paid for such good wines.

Baron Philippe thus had at least good quality to start his carrier as a wine producer, but little else. He was, however, unhappy about the fifth position in the rating and set about to change this. With measures to improve the quality of the wines even further, and with proper marketing, it did not take him long to achieve prices in line, or even better, than his first growth rivals. Part of the success in obtaining better prices was, no doubt, his decision in 1924 to bottle his wine at the Chateau, a practice which caused consternation among the Bordeaux wine traders, but which was soon copied by all the top estates. Good public relations work did the rest. Credit must surely go to the Baron for raising Ch. Mouton-Rothschild by the government decree of 1973 to the status of 'Premier Grand Cru Classé du Medoc'. At that time Monsieur Jacques Chirac was France's Minister of Agriculture, later to become President of France. The Baron's comment: "First I am; second I was; Mouton doesn't change".

This was by no means Baron Philippe de Rothschild's only achievement. To sell the wines of the disastrous vintages 1930, 1931 and 1932 (none were of Mouton standard) he launched the appellation 'Bordeaux' wine 'Mouton Cadet', a selection of sound wines blended for this marque which is now selling in huge quantities.

In 1933 he bought Ch. Mouton d'Armailhacq and in 1970 Ch.Clerk-Milon (now known as 'Mouton-Baronne Pauline', in honour of his second wife who died in 1976). Together with Baroness Pauline de Rothschild he established the museum at Chateau Mouton-Rothschild which houses many ancient and modern exhibits. Much later, he encouraged Robert Mondavi of the Napa Valley, California, to start a joint venture which culminated in 1981 with the release of 'Opus One' of the 1979 vintage, the first of a series of great California Cabernet Sauvignon (see also Stephen Spurrier).

In his book ´Mouton-Rothschild - the wine, the family, the museum´ (1980), Cyril Ray has given a more detailed account of Baron Philippe de Rothschild's outstanding career.

Louis M. Martini Sr.

The Italian winemaker, Louis M. Martini Sr. founded his California winery, near St Helena, in 1922. In his ´World Atlas of Wine´ Hugh Johnson describes it as "the most distinguished winery in California".
Louis M. Martini was ready in 1933, just after the Repeal of the prohibition law, to launch his California wines on the market. His philosophy was simple but effective: "Provide the customer the best possible quality at the lowest manageable price".

With California and Sonoma grapes made into wine by an expert winemaker, the quality was excellent. The price must have been right too, because his wines were at one point considered the best value for money in the world. The Cabernet Sauvignon and Chardonnay wines are still thought of as some of the best in California, and although Martini sold his wines early, most of them had longevity and matured to great wines for which he is remembered beyond his time.

Louis Martini Sr. died aged 87 in 1974, but his son Louis Martini carries on the tradition.

Wilhelm Möslinger

At the beginning of the 20th century wine production became more technical. Wine drinkers expected bottled wines without faults, both in quality and appearance. Filters have been developed so that clear wine could always be provided. However, more technology meant more metallic utensils and machinery with the result that wine acids partly dissolved such metals as iron, copper and zinc. With oxygen, phosphates and tannins this led to insoluble compounds which appeared as a haze or deposits in the bottle.

Dr. Wilhelm Möslinger, a research chemist in Neustadt (Germany) experimented with finings, and in 1923 the German government approved the 'Möslinger' fining, i.e. the addition to wine of potassium ferrocyanide which, with iron, formed 'prussian blue' which is removed, and the treatment became generally known as 'blue fining'.

Blue fining was not approved in all countries, but it was widely used by chemists and oenologists simply because they had no other means to deal with the excess metal problem. It was and is essential; however, that blue fining is applied under the supervision of an experienced chemist or oenologist.

With stainless steel and polyester being used nowadays, metal contamination is practically eliminated and blue fining is seldom needed.

Albert Bürklin

The 'Weingut Dr. Bürklin-Wolf' at Wachenheim is Germany's largest private wine grower. The two families

Bürklin and Wolf are on record of having owned vineyards in Wachenheim since the time of the Elector Karl Theodor. In 1875 Johann Ludwig Wolf´s granddaughter married Dr. Albert Bürklin and thus the properties were united.

From 1924 to 1979 the estate was managed by Dr. Albert Bürklin, a co-founder of the ´German Viticultural Association´. He made some of the finest wines in Germany. His widow Jutta carried on the tradition and now their daughter, a graduate of Geisenheim, is at the helm of this excellent estate.

Max Chapoutier

The Chapoutier family of Tain, in the heart of the Rhone Valley wine district of France, where the world's greatest red wines from the Syrah grape are made, have made wine since 1808. This is now the oldest wine grower and merchant in the Rhone Valley, and Max Chapoutier made it one of the largest and successful.

Max Chapoutier came into the business around the early thirties, aged 23, following in the footsteps of his grandfather Marius and father Marc. Their pride and joy is the 77 acre vineyard on the famous ´Hermitage Hill´. Max acquired the 66 acre ´Domaine de la Bernadine´ in Châteauneuf-du-Pape, 15 acres at Croizes-Hermitage and a small holding at Côte-Rotie. As if this was not enough, he also promoted the rosé wines of Tavel.

Maynard A. Amerine

This viticulturist, oenologist and author was educated at the University of California where he obtained his B.Sc. in

1932 and his Ph. D. in plant physiology in 1936. He was professor of enology and as chairman of the 'Department of Viticulture and Enology' at Davis from 1935 through to 1974 was one of the pioneers of enology as well as a prolific writer with more technical books on wine to his credit than any other. Together with A. J. Winkler he further developed Eugene Hilgard's heat summation theory that relates climatic conditions to the composition and quality of grapes and of wine. This practical guide enables wine growers to select the grape variety best suited to given climatic conditions.

Leon D. Adams

Just before the prohibition ended in 1933 Leon Adams, a graduate of the University of California, organised the 'Grape Growers League of California' to promote the production and consumption of table wines in preference to the consumption of hard liquor. The Grape Growers League is the forerunner of what became the 'Wine Institute', which Adams served as secretary for twenty years.

In 1938 he also launched the 'Wine Advisory Board' with the 'California Department of Agriculture'. He later retired from the Wine Institute to become a full time wine writer and lecturer with many important publications to his credit.

Ernest and Julio Gallo

In 1933 the Gallo Brothers established what has become the world's largest winery. The headquarters and main winery are in Modesto in the San Joaquin Valley (Central

Valley), to the east of San Francisco with many more vineyards and wineries in other parts of California.

The dimensions of the Modesto complex on some 30 acres of land are comparable to an oil refinery. The winery with its 4,600 employees has a huge storage and blending capacity with just one tank holding a million gallons of wine. It has its own bottle factory, and when I visited Ernest and Julio Gallo, there were about 30 bottling lines with supporting laboratories and any number of graduates from the University of California, many of whom have since become well known, if not famous, wine makers in their own right. At one point Gallo had a 60% share of the American market with distribution centers in most countries around the world.

Most of the wines Gallo sells are good jug wines, attractively packaged and priced. In recent years inroads have also been made in the premium wine market by buying estates in the Napa Valley and elsewhere, with vineyards for which literally mountains have been moved to improve the soil and exposure to the sun. Oak (cask) cellars have been built to mature the premium Cabernet Sauvignons and Chardonnays.

Earnest and Julio Gallo were not just pioneer wine makers of California, they were legends in their own lifetime with many envious critics. Julio Gallo died in a car accident in 1993 and his brother Ernest died 2007 at the age of 97.

Harry Waugh

It is amazing what a person can achieve with a good palate, a matching memory and determination, even in the ´respectable´ wine trade, which in those days only employed young men who moved in the 'right circles' with an education at Harrow, Oxford or Cambridge.

Harry Waugh started in the wine trade in 1934, at the age of 30, as a clerk with a London wine merchant. Later, with the fashionable 'Block Grey and Block'. When his skills could no longer be overlooked, he was invited to take part in tastings to assess wines and spirits for their potential qualities. After the Second World War he joined 'Harveys of Bristol' where he soon became wine buyer and director. He specialised in clarets and burgundies. Later he was even invited to become a director of the famous 'Chateau Latour' of Bordeaux.

Harry Waugh is considered to have one of the best palates in the wine trade, and since 1966 he has been a wine consultant, wine writer - with many books to his credit - and is a co-founder of the 'Zinfandel Club'. He was one of the first to recognise the potential of the new generation of California wines. He became wine consultant to Her Majesty Queen Elizabeth II, 'Les Amis du Vin', the Ritz Hotels, and a director of the 'International Wine and Spirit Competition'.

With all his achievements Harry Waugh remained a modest person. When asked the catching question:
"Have you ever mistaken a burgundy for a claret?"
he responded: "not since lunch!"

Georges Faively and Camille Rodier

In 1934 they founded the famous wine fraternity 'La Confrerie des Chevalier du Tastevin' to promote the wines of Burgundy.

Erwin Wanner

Dr. Erwin Wanner was the head of the research institute of viticulture and horticulture at Geisenheim, Germany from 1934 to 1939. He was active in teaching and researched the practical application of measures to enhance the making and treatment of wine.For this work he designed the Geisenheim-Viewing-Cask (oak cask with glass ends) so that the effect of finings and clarifying agents added to wine could be observed.

From 1947 to 1958 he was the principle director of the viticultural and agricultural research and teaching centre Bad Kreuznach, Germany. During this time he developed, with Wilhelm Geiss, chief chemsit of the Seitz Werke, Bad Kreuznach, controlled fermentations in pressure tanks. This enables wine makers to opt for slow fermentations. Fermentations can also be stopped under pressure to retain unfermented sugar for improved wine quality.

Brother Timothy

The Christan Brothers, a religious lay teaching order, was founded in Reims, France, in 1680 and has grown to 18,000 members in 86 countries. The order came to California in 1868 and planted vineyards to make sacramental wine and wine for their own table. Any surplus wine was sold.

In 1932 their new premises in the Napa Valley were occupied, and in 1935 Brother Timothy F.S.C ((Frates Scholarium Christianarum) was appointed to the important post of cellar master. The now famous ´Mont La Salle´ vineyard, eventually extending to some 360 acres, was planted. The best known and most successful wine is undoubtedly the cold fermented ´Pineau de la Loire´ (made from the French Chenin Blanc grape).

The Christian Brothers also own the ´Champagne Cellars´ at St. Helena with 700 acres and the ´Mount Tivy Winery´ near Reedley with 1000 acres. The estates now produce a full range of sparkling, vintage and fortified wines.

Brother Timothy has won more prizes for his wines than any other cellarmaster of his time.

Gerhard Troost

Gerhard Troost was an oenologist in every sense of the word. After attending the wine school at Geisenheim (Germany) he became a technical assistant at the Botanical Institute and from 1937 to 1939 he was an assitant teacher for oenology at the Institute of Viticulture and Kellerwirtschaft. After the war he lectured on wine making, which included practical courses. His motto: theory must prove its worth in practice.

In 1971 the Geisenheim Institute was re-organised. The Ingenieurschule became the Fachhochschule attached to the University of Wiesbaden and Gerhard Troost was appointed Professor of Oenology and Beverage Technology. His book *Die Technologie des Weines (1955)* also referred to as the wine technology bible, was, next to Babo and Mach's *Handbuch des Weines und der Kellerwirtschaft (1910),* the most comprehensive book on the subject of oenology and ran to many editions.

André Tschelinstcheff

André Tschelinstcheff, Russian born, was educated at the ´Moscow University´, the ´Institute of Agricultural Technology´ in Czechoslovakia and the ´National

Agronomy' in France. He came to California in 1938 to help shape the fortunes of Beaulieu Vineyard, where he was active for more than thirty years. He also became one of the most influential oenological consultants to some of the then best known wine estates and was affectionately called 'the wine maker's winemaker'.

He also pioneered the Cabernet Sauvignon grape in the Napa Valley. André Tschelinstcheff was undoubtedly a pioneer who helped to create the new generation of California wines that captured the world markets.

Lenz Moser

Dr. Lenz Moser of Rohrendorf, Austria, experimented with a new system of training vines with the aim of reducing labour costs in vineyards by using tractors for cultivation and spraying, to improve yields and quality by providing better air circulation within the vine foliage and thus reduce attacks of peronospera and oidium etc. To reduce spring frost damage he raised the trellises.

By 1940 he had achieved his ambitions and his 'high culture system' was adopted over the years by 60% to 80% of the Austrian wine growers. Many wine growers in other countries copied or adapted his system to local conditions.

The basic change from traditional vineyards was to widen the rows to about 3 or 3.5 meters with gaps between the vines, within the rows 1.25 meters and the first wire at a height of some 1.25 meters above ground.

In his book 'Weinbau einmal anders' (1966) Dr. Moser explains fully his high culture system. He became a legend in his own lifetime and was especially well regarded in Austria.

Paul Alfons Fürst von Metternich

Schloss Johannisberg is Germany´s foremost Riesling estate producing outstanding wines since the days of the Emperor Charlmagne (768-814 AD) who had noticed, from his palace at Ingelheim on the other side of the Rhine that the snow melted on this paticular spot earlier than elsewhere. He decreed that a vineyard be plantd there and his son Ludwig harvested the first crop of 6,000 litres wine in 817.

The Bendictine monks from Mainz built the first monastery and in 1130 a Romanesque basilica was consecrated in honour of St.John the Baptist and thus the mountain and the village became known as Johannisberg. Johannisberg was administered by several clerical institutions and in 1716 the Baron of Fulda purchased the estate and started the construction of the baroque palace. In 1720 the first Riesling vines were planted so that Schloss Johannisberg is the oldest Riesling vineyard in the world. The name ´Johannisberg Riesling´ is used as a synonym for Riesling vines in many new-world regions.

At Schloss Johannisberg the term Spätlese (late harvest) was first used and this resulted from the late arrival of a messenger from Fulda giving permission for the 1775 harvest to commence. The messenger arrived so late that the grapes had started to rot but the resultant wine was excellent. Ten years later it was discovered that grapes affected by this ´noble´ rot (botrytis cinearea) was beneficial because water was extracted from the grapes and a very attractive flavour was added. The resultant wines

were called Auslese (selected late harvest). Later came the even more selectively harvested Beerenauslese, Trockenbeerenauslese and Eiswein, the latter being made with frozen grapes from which even more concentrated grape juice was
extracted.

In 1806 Napoleon aquired the estate. In 1816 the Emperor Frank I presented it to his trusted Chancellor Clemens Wenzeslaus L. Fürst von Metternich for services rendered during the Napoleonoc wars.

Paul Alfons von Metternich, great grandson of the famous Chancellor, inherited Schloss Johannisberg which was bombed and largely destroyed in 1942. After the war he began the daunting task of re-building this enormous estate and restored it to its former glory., not just in terms of building structures but also its reputation as a producer of some of the finest Riesling wines the world has come to appreciate.

The main features that led to the production of the exceptional Johannisberg Riesling wines are the predominantly chist and quarzite soil, the clon selected Riesling vines, the large cask wine cellars (vaults dating back to 1721) that provide ideal storage conditions, and of course the great care during vinification and the maturation of the bottled wines. Johannisberg has some 85 acres of vineyards with 100% Riesling vines that surround the estate.

Joseph Heitz

Joe Heitz, a graduate of the University of California, came to the Napa Valley in 1944. He gained practical experience at the ´Gallo Winery´ in Modesto, the ´Wine Growers

Guild´ in Lodi, and at ´Mission Bell´ in Madera before he became assistant to the famous André Tchelinstcheff.

In 1961, as one of the first new generation oenologists he started, from scratch, his own very modest winery without the help of financial partners. He bought what is now known as the ´Tasting Room´ with a few acres of vineyard on Highway 29, south of St. Helena. To finance his venture he handled wines from other growers, and he bought grapes from others to make his own wines.

His reputation as winemaker was established, when he made the then best California red wine from Cabernet Sauvignon grapes grown in the now legendary ´Martha´s Vineyard´. Chardonnay from the ´Hazell Vineyard´ established his reputation also as a white wine maker. His wines reached hitherto unknown prices and this laid the foundation for expansion. In 1964 he and his wife bought the ´Old Stone Winery´ at Taplin Road, with more vineyards, along the Silverado Trail, now the family home and main cellar.

Joe Heitz at one time, was considered the best winemaker of California.

Alexis Lichine

Born in Russia, Alexis Lichine arrived in the United States in his teens via Paris. During the Second World War he served in the US army and became protocol aide-de-camp for General Eisenhauer.

In the 1950´s he bought, with a group of investors, the Bordeaux ´Chateau Cantenac Prieure´ (later renamed Chateau Prieure-Lichine) and ´Chateaux Lascomes´. In

1955 he founded Alexis Lichine and Co., a successful wine shipping company and he became a well known writer and promoter of French wines in the United States.

His book ´Alexis Lichine´s Encyclopedia of Wines and Spirits´ was published in 1967 and has sold over 250,000 copies. This is a remarkable achievement, because it is a tome of about 700 pages.

1950 AD - 2000 AD

The making of quality wine probably peaked during the 1950's and 1960's. In 1961 the best ever Bordeaux wines were probably made and Burgundy and Germany had such exceptionally good vintages as 1959 and 1971. Excellent wines are still being harvested in good vintages, but prices for the really good estate wines are too high for many a wine lover.

Technology, used prudently, made it possible to protect the grapes, until the ideal time for harvesting came and modern presses, fermentation vessels, laboratory quality control procedures, cask maturation, where appropriate, and hygienic bottling had been perfected to achieve excellence and lasting quality.

Later, technological advances, however, also had their negative influence. Wines with ever shorter maturation periods could be made with the help of oak shavings instead of expensive oak casks. Reverse-osmosis to extract water from grape juice prior to fermentation made it possible to adjust the sugar/alcohol/acidity levels in poor vintages and sugar additions (Chaptalisation) allows wines to be stretched.

Globalisation brought us the flying winemaker who can make wine around the globe to his specifications so that ´uniwines´ are now on offer no matter where the wine comes from. Supermarkets gave wine merchants little chance to compete on equal terms. The buying power of conglomerates in turn, led to oenologists having to make wines to their specifications and supply them at their prices. This state of affairs left little room for enterprising young wine makers, and even established wine estates had, to some degree, to follow this trend. Far too many young wines, often to the point of being undrinkable, when overoaked, were offered to the unsuspecting public.

Fortunately many pioneer growers and wine makers have survived, against all the odds. It is good to see that quality wine making gradually returns on a broader scale; and merchants, who can offer these good wines to discerning wine drinkers, are once again flourishing.

Miguel Torres

Although the Torres roots as wine makers go back to 1870, its fame started in the early 1950's, when the two Torres, a father and son team by the same name, took a new approach to wine making in the north-eastern Spanish region of Penedes.

Miguel Torres sent his son Miguel Augustin to Dijon, France to study viticulture and wine making, and with that knowledge and much hard work to learn all he could in other parts of the world, he set about to grow grapes like the white Chardonnay, Sauvignon Blanc, Riesling, Gewuerztraminer and the red Cabernet Sauvignon and Pinot Noir. In the vineyards he introduced new pruning and training systems to improve quality at the expense of quantity. It took several decades to convince his compatriots, who grow the grapes in their own vineyards, that only quality could bring economic success in the long term.

By the time Miguel A.Torres took control of the bodega in 1951, after his father's death, he had introduced the most modern wine making technology using stainless steel tanks, cold fermentation and all that was required to yield the best possible quality from the improved grapes that were harvested.

Miguel's efforts were a blueprint for wine makers in other parts of Spain, and Torres is now the largest family owned wine estate in Spain. Miguel did not stop there. With his able brother Jaime - who looked after the interests at the Vilafranca del Penedes bodega - he found time to establish a 220 hectar wine estate in Curió, Chile, and his sister Marimar (who studied Enology and Viticulture at the University of California, Davis) is in charge of marketing Torres wines in the USA. She also established a winery with 60 hectares vineyards in Sonoma, California, that produces 15,000 cases of top quality Chardonnay and Pinot Noir each vintage.

Marquis de Goulaine

Muscadet, the French, Loire white wine, received its appellations controlées 'Muscadet de Sevre et Maine' and 'Coteaux de la Loire' in 1936, but it was not until the 1950's that the wines attracted attention after they became available in a standardised, reliable quality.

One of the pioneers to make the wine so popular was Robert, 11th Marquis de Goulaine, who resides in his ancestral home, the Chateaux de Goulaine, at Goulaine near Nantes. His Chateaux, with some 100 acres of top quality vineyards, makes some of the best Muscadet sur Lie (bottled unfiltered, off the lees). Only about 150,000 bottles of this excellent wine from the Muscadet (Melon de Bourgogne) grape is made annually. The quality of this wine is only surpassed by Goullaine's own 'Cuveé du Millionaire', with sales limited to 15,000 bottles.

Wilhelm Geiss

Wilhelm Geiss, wine chemist, was for many years head of the research laboratory at the wine research and teaching institute of Bad Kreuznach, Germany. In 1950 he was appointed chief chemist of the research laboratory, Seitz Werke, Bad Kreuznach, where he and the Seitz engineers developed equipment for cold sterile bottling of wine. Cold sterile bottling is worldwide the preferred method for quality table wines with residual sugar which were previously stabilised with chemicals (sulphur dioxide or sorbic acid) flash pasteurisation or hot bottling all of which proved unsatisfactory.

Sir Guy Salisbury-Jones

In 1952 Major General Sir Guy Salisbury-Jones, GCVO, CMG, CBE, MC, inspired by the writings of Edward Hyams and Ray Barrington Brock, planted the first commercial vineyard in England since Lord Bute's vineyard at Castel Coch near Cardiff was abandoned in 1920. Sir Guy planted 3½ acres at Hambledon, Hampshire, with the French hybrid Seyve-Villard 5/276 and the vineyard was later extended with Chardonnay and Pinot Noir. The soil at Hambledon being chalky, the wine is more in the style of still Champagne or crisp Loire, rather than Hock or Moselle.

In 1958 Robert and Margaret Gore-Browne planted a five acre vineyard on Lord Montague's estate at Beaulieu, also in Hampshire, where they used Müller-Thurgau, Seyve-Villard and Wrotham Pint (Pinot Meunier), the latter for colour to make rosé wine. The quality of Hambledon and Beaulieu wines was good to very good, and the national media soon reported on these successful ventures. Many more vineyards were planted throughout England and Wales.

By 1967 vine plantings had gathered pace to such an extent, that it was thought advisable to form an association to represent the interests of the many commercial growers and to set quality standards. The inaugural meeting was held at my offices at Ockley, Surrey. The founder members were: Sir Guy Salisbury-Jones (President), Irene Barrett, Norman Cowderoy, Robin Don, Lady Montague of Beaulieu, Jack Ward and Philip Tyson-Woodcock, with myself as technical adviser.

Hugh Barty-King reported full details on the revival of English viticulture in his thoroughly researched book ´A Tradition of English Wine´ (1977).

Max Schubert

Penfolds Wines was founded in 1844 by the English medical Doctor Christopher Rawson-Penfold, near his home, Grange Cottage, in Adelaide, South Australia.

However, it was the winemaker Max Schubert who brought fame to Penfolds when he, supported by Jeff Penfold Hyland, literally re-invented Australian red wine production. He did what the Bordelaise had done long before, mature wines in small oak casks. Max Schubert, however, used the Rhone grape Shiraz or Syrah which is known in Australia as Hermitage. It was widely planted in Australia for the production of Port style wines. In addition to Shiraz, it is thought, that a small percentage of Cabernet Sauvignon was also used.

In 1953 and in 1955 Max Schubert made his first great vintages of 'Penfold's Grange Hermitage'. At first Schubert earned nothing but criticism from colleagues in the wine trade and from customers, who had not understood his aim to produce a wine that would mature for 20 years or more and should not be judged prematurely. The efforts bore fruit in the long run with the Penfolds Grange Hermitage, time and again, being rated the best and most expensive of all Australian wines.

There were, however, variations from vintage to vintage, depending on where the grapes came from, which oak was chosen, how much new oak was used and how long the wine was kept in casks. Gradually he settled on American oak, in which the wine matured up to 18 months.

The grapes came, according to Len Evans, essentially from five vineyards, Magill, Morphett Vale, Kalimna, Clare and Koonunga Hill. This prolific author and Australian wine expert provides tasting notes for many of the Grange Hermitage vintages, with a list showing the percentage of grapes from the various vineyards for the vintages from 1951 to 1980, in his book 'Len Evans' Complete Book of Australian Wine' (1984).

Pierre Galet

Professor Galet published between 1956 and 1964 his four volume work 'Cepages et Vignobles de France', an ampelography describing, for the first time, features of the young shoots and leaves, and not just the fruit clusters for the exact identification of European vine varieties and root stocks. This is the most comprehensive ampelography which was translated, updated and enlarged to include vines grown in the United States and Canada by his

American student Lucy T. Morton. This English version was published in 1978 under the title 'A Practical Ampelography'.

Miljenko Grgich

Miljenko Grgich, a Croatian oenologist, who studied at the University of Zagreb, came to California in 1958.

He worked for the Christian Brothers, Beaulieu Vineyard as well as André Tchelistcheff and Robert Mondavi before he joined 'Chateau Montelina Winery'. He became famous, practically overnight, when in 1976 - at the famous Paris tasting (organised by Stephen Spurrier), - his 1973 Montelina Chardonnay came first against some of the best white Burgundies.

In 1977 Grgich left Montelina to start his own Grgich Hills Cellars north of Rutherford.

Wolf Blass

In 1961 Wolf Blass, a German Kellermeister and trained sparkling winemaker, arrived in Australia via England.

His skills and showmanship made him famous in the wine world and one of the richest men in Australia. He arrived at a good time in the Barrossa Valley when the hitherto rather dull Australian wine trade started to wake up to innovation.

Between 1960 and 1969 consumption of wine rose by 60%. Wolf left the 'Kaiser Stuhl' winery in 1964 to start his own company and work as a freelance winemaker-consultant. In 1966 he started selling his own Bilyara label wine. In 1973 he took the final step to independence, and a huge success story began.

His wines won all the major awards. By 1990 he had won 145 trophies, 769 gold medals, 880 silver medals and 956 bronze medals, among them the coveted Jimmy Watson Trophy, IWSC gold, silver and bronze medals etc. This resulted in a huge demand for these highly praised wines and appropriate profits for the many wine companies he had founded or acquired. By 1984 he took the company to the stock exchange, with a capitalisation of $15,700,000, and ultimately the South Australian Brewing Company could not resist and bought the Wolf Blass enterprise for more than ten times this sum on condition that he, the master winemaker and marketing man extraordinaire, remains on board.

Max Lake

US born Max Lake has lived in Australia from early childhood. He had an extraordinary career as a surgeon and winemaker, who also published a handful of wine books, and he researched flavours with emphasis on wine.

In his own vineyard ´Lake´s Folly´, in the Hunter Valley, planted in 1963, he made outstanding wines from the French classics Cabernet Sauvignon and Chardonnay.

In 1986 Dr. Lake was President of the ´International Wine & Spirit Competition´ (London) where he impressed everyone with his knowledge of wine and with his own wines which had reached perfection.

Warren Winiarski

Warren Winiarski and his wife Barbara left teaching jobs at the University of Chicago in 1964 to start their new vocation as wine growers and wine makers in California. Before they started their 'Stag's Leap Wine Cellars' on the Silverado Trail in the Napa Valley he jobbed with other wine makers to learn all he could.

Warren Winiarski is a perfectionist and artist who spends much of his time in the vineyard with his vines to get the feel of the crop as the grapes ripen, and thus he can adjust his vintaging to the prevailing conditions. Already the third crop from his 45 acre vineyard brought him an early success when, at the famous 1976 Paris tasting (organised by Stephen Spurrier), his 'Stag's Leap 1973 Cabernet Sauvignon' won the first prize against some of the great Bordeaux vintages. Winiarski's methodical approach to wine making soon yielded also some of the best Napa Valley Chardonnays.

Warren Winiarski did much for the new generation of California wines and which, in effect, started a new gold rush with many of the world market leaders wanting to own vineyards in northern California and to make their fortunes there.

Alan Rook

Major Alan Rook, a Nottingham wine merchant and former chairman of the Wine and Spirit Association of Great Britain, planted in 1964 the probably worlds most northerly vineyard. His estate, Stragglethorpe Hall, once a 12th century monastery, is situated in Linconshire on the 53rd paralell.

The vineyard comprises 1.5 acres and produces about two thousand bottles 'Lincoln
Imperial' a dry white wine from Mueller-Thurgau and Seyve-Villard vines. In his book *The Diary of an English Vineyard (1969)* published by Wine & Spirit Publications Ltd. (1969), Alan Rook describes in great detail how he set about growing the grapes and making the wine.

Michael Broadbent

Michael Broadbent appeared in the limelight of the English wine scene when, in 1966, he joined the famous London auction house ´Christie´s´ to re-start their wine auctions. Before that, he was a director of ´Harveys of Bristol´, and he became one of the first ´Masters of Wine´.

His book ´Wine Tasting´, first published in 1968, has seen numerous reprints and up-dates, and has become a sort of bible to wine students and wine enthusiasts alike.

There is no doubt that Michael Broadbent made a great success of the wine auctions for which he was responsible until the 1990´s. During his time at Christie´s he also initiated the publication of many interesting books on various aspects of wine and of some leading wine personalities.

Hans Ambrosi

The ´Staatsdomäne of Hesse´ (Eltville, Rheingau) with its six estates and a total of 189 hectares vineyards is the largest wine producer in Germany. The medieval monastery, ´Kloster Eberbach´, the jewel in the crown, was confiscated during the Napoleonic period in 1803 and was given to the Duke of Nassau.

As early as 1730 one of the old cellars was given the name 'Kabinett', where especially good vintages were stored and thus the term 'Kabinett', still used today to describe good quality German wines, was born.

For 35 years, since 1966, Dr. Ambrosi has been the director in charge at Eltville. He was the innovator par excellence, who introduced the now famous wine tastings, a wine fair and the 'German Wine Academy'. He also developed the wine auctions, which had been started in 1806.

Kloster Eberbach and the monastery attracts thousands of visitors each year. Despite its impressive size and diversity, Dr. Ambrosi has achieved a very high standard of quality for the many individual wines that are produced. In the Rheingau, naturally, the Riesling is almost exclusively planted, and for red wine production - in the slatey soil of Assmannshausen - the Pinot Noir is used.

Apart from his task of managing this enormous enterprise, Dr. Ambrosi has found time to write several books on German wines, and some have been translated into English.

Robert Mondavi

In California, Robert Mondavi, who had left the Charles Krug winery which his father Cesare had established and which, after long legal battles, is now run by his brother Peter, started his own winery at Oakville in 1966.

From the beginning Robert (Bob) Mondavi was convinced that the wines of the Napa Valley would one day become the world's most sought after - and he was right. His motto was: "To Strive, to Seek, to Find". He travelled to Europe year after year to find out how the great wines were made. He planted his vineyards with the classical varieties Cabernet Sauvignon, Merlot, Pinot Noir, Chardonnay, Sauvignon Blanc, and he experimented with oak cask maturation and much more. He worked with the great scientists Professors M. A. Amerine, H. W. Berg, W. V. Cruess, Eugene Hilgard, M. A. Joslyn, V. L. Singleton and A. J. Winkler, etc. of the University of California, Davis, and he co-operated with his fellow California vineyard owners/wine makers Charles Carpi, Mike Grgich, Joseph Heitz, Joseph Phelps, Andre Tschelistcheff, Warren Winiarsky, and many more. His reputation grew to such an extent, especially after the 1976 Paris tasting, that the Europeans took notice (See also Stephen Spurrier). The Mondavi Winery is now effectively run by Robert´s sons Michael and Tim and daughter Marcia.

In his book ´Robert Mondavi of the Napa Valley´ (1984), Cyril Ray summerised Robert´s achievements in a very expert and readable manner.

Giacomo Tachis

Dr. Giacomo Tachis is one of the best known and respected Italian wine makers who, from the late sixties onwards, experimented with the Cabernet Sauvignon grape.

Although he was born in Piemonte, he became known as the creator of the famous ´Tignanello´, a wine made with Cabernet Sauvignon in barriques at the Tuscan ´Sassicaia´ estate in Bolgheri, owned by the Marchese Mario Incesa.

Tachis was also the winemaker for the Marchese Piero Antiori (in who's cellars the Tignanello was bottled), and other consultants were Professor Emile Peynoud of Bordeaux and Luigi Veronelli (in those days considered to be the 'high priest' of Italian fine wine). Thus the first Chianti with some Cabernet Sauvignon, and without white grapes, was born.

Marchese Piero Antinori

The House of Antinori are among the oldest wine growers and merchants in Tuscany, dating back to the fourteenth century, when the family was enrolled in the 'Guild of Merchants' and became wine and olive merchants with their own orchards and vineyards. The present Marchese Piero Antinori carries on the tradition.

With his courageous decision to introduce - in the 1960's,- Cabernet Sauvignon to his cépage, he has broken with tradition and is marketing his wines without the blessing of the Chianti Classico DOC. He and many other wine experts, including, of course, his winemaker Giacomo Tachis, who is thought to have led the way in this movement, are convinced that the quality of the new style of Chianti with Cabernet Sauvignon and without white grapes in the blend, is a considerable improvement to latter day standards.

Richard Peterson

The oenologist Dr. Richard (Dick) Peterson joined the Coca Cola owned 'Monterey Vineyard' around 1970 after working with Gallo and with Andre Tschelinstcheff at Beaulieu Vineyards. Richard Peterson is one of the most innovative winemakers in California.

At Gonzales, Monterey County, the vines are grown in north California's coolest regions and provide intense varietal character, with good acidity, through a long ripening season. Peterson makes the best of these features.

In 1974 and 1975 he produced what was then probably the best Pinot Noir in California, and his famous ´December harvest´ of Zinfandel made the headlines time and again. Bortrytis is also developing on the grapes to make excellent Johannisberg Riesling dessert wine.

Another first and probably the only wine of its kind in the USA is the ´early harvest´ or ´extremely early harvest´ nouveau style wine made from the true Beaujolais Gamay grapes grown in, for example, 1978, but harvested in early January 1979. The wine was made by the 'maceration carbonique' method and was sold as a novelty in the summer of 1979.

Dick Peterson is also a master at making traditional wines from other grapes, his Cabernet Sauvignon and Chardonnay being rated ´second to none´.

Stephen Spurrier

The California wine makers have known for a long time that their wines could challenge the best of Europe, and a few European wine experts, among them Harry Waugh and Michael Broadbent, had also recognised that potential, especially of the Napa Valley wines.

In the 1972 International Wine & Spirit Competition Father Timothy's Christian Bros. Chenin Blanc 1971 won a gold medal in 1973; the 1972, again, won gold a year later. Some of the other leading wine makers at this breakthrough time for California wines were: Miljenko Grgich, Joseph Heitz, Louis M. Martin, Robert Mondavi, Richard Peterson, André Tschelininstcheff and Warren Winiarsky.

On 24th May 1976, Stephen Spurrier, the Englishman who owns 'Les Caves de la Madeleine'- a well known Paris wine merchants business and the private 'Académie du Vin' decided to organise a blind tasting of Chardonnays (the grape that makes the finest white Burgundies) and Cabernet Sauvignons (the outstanding Bordeaux grape) to compare the wines made from these grapes in California and France. It was supposed to be an educational event, to draw attention to the celebration of the 'Bicentenary Declaration of Independence' of 1776, and to get publicity for his Wine Academie.

Only the best vitages available at the time were selected, and the tasting was scrupulously blind and fair, although only French experts were invited to evaluate the wines. The 1973 Chateau Montelena Chardonnay, with Miljenko Grgich the winemaker, and the 1973 Stag's Leap Cabernet Sauvignon, made by Warren Winniarsky, were the respective winners. This result was most upsetting for the French wine community, and certainly put California on the world wine map, and deservedly so - not because the California wines were judged to be better than their French counterparts - but because California wines are of good quality in their own right. The wines of both countries are excellent, but different. California wines appeal with powerful flavours and lots of alcohol (and consequently with more mouth filling glycerine) whereas the French have more subtle flavours which take time to develop in the glass and in comparative tasting this time is not always given.

Following these successes, California came into the international lime-light, with many of the leading wine companies wanting to share in the prospects that were evident.

One of the most spectacular ´joint ventures´ was between Baron Philippe de Rothschild and Robert Mondavi, who announced in 1980, that they would produce jointly a California Cabernet Sauvignon, later named ´Opus One´. The wine makers Tim Mondavi and Lucien Sioneau of Chateau Mouton Rothschild made the wine at the Mondavi, Oakville winery from grapes grown in their Napa Valley vineyards. Later the new company bought land and planted their own vines.

The first 5000 cases of ´Opus One 1979´ (a blend of 80% Cabernet Sauvignon, 16% Cabernet Franc and 4% Merlot) were released in the spring of 1981 and fetched astronomical prices, as may have been expected. In later vintages the proportion of Cabernet Sauvignon was increased.

About the author

Anton Massel came to England in 1956 from Germany as a qualified oenologist (Ingenieur grad.) to take charge of the service laboratory of the then Seitz UK agents in London. Seitz are the famous German manufacturers of wine handling equipment, the pioneer of wine filtration and cold sterile bottling which has become the standard procedure for quality wines.

In 1960 Anton established his own laboratory in the city of London where, as an independent consultant, he analysed wines and spirits for British wine shippers, bottlers and English wine growers. Until the Wine & Spirit Education Trust was founded in 1968 he also organised lecture courses on viticulture at Sir Guy Salisbury Jone's Hambledon Vineyards and on wine making and wine handling in his own laboratories in London and Ockley. In 1976 he was elected a 'Professional Member' of the American Society of Enologists.

Analysing wines and spirits and assessing their quality and stability, however, was day to day work and with so many UK wine shippers and merchants having contacts abroad it was only a matter of time before the idea to find out where the best wines and spirits come from became reality.

In 1969, as part of the activities of Club Oenologique Ltd., a wine appreciation club, he organised the first International Wine & Spirit Competition (IWSC). International tasting panels and, for the first time, chemical analysis, to ensure that no hidden problems – which organoleptic examination would not neccessarily detect – were used to assess the quality of entries. Gas Chromatography equipment was relatively expensive at that time, but when the Austrian glycol scandal

(1985) came upon us; it saved the embarrassment of possibly awarding prizes to doctored wines.

Kathleen Bourke, (then editor of 'Wine Magazine') wrote the introduction to the 1975 competition results booklet. She put the merits of the IWSC this way:

"A Tribute to the International Wine and Spirits Competition.

For centuries England has held a special place in the world of wine. You would think that a country that in the past centuries produced little or no wine would keep quiet about the subject. Not so. Modestly, unassumingly, we undertook from the beginning to teach our grandmother to suck eggs – or to sip wine – confident that we knew. Actually, we did.

Our wine merchants travelled, and still do, far afield to bring to our shores the best wines from all the wine-producing districts of the world. Indeed in many instances with the same modesty, these same merchants invented wine- whoever heard of the Portuguese producing, let alone drinking, Port until merchants persuaded them to make the wine and helped them to develop their trade?

The English love of claret and hock played a big part in the development of those wines in Bordeaux and the Rhineland. The palate of the English consumer and the expertise and skills, the enterprise of our merchants made the seal of approval of the English a highly desirable thing.

As a mighty Empire, the English could be somewhat autocratic: today as a small compact nation, we can yet keep our standards, and indeed we do. We are still the great entrepot for the world wine trade, witness the unique London wine auctions to which the best wines flow from every part of the country and from which they are dispatched to every part of the globe.

Anton Massel, a German oenologist, whom I have known for many years and respected for his knowledge, his enterprise and his exceeding hard work, is today contributing to this international fame of ours. For many years, as founder and chairman of Club Oenologique he has worked to keep the international line open. He has undoubtedly added a further dimension to England's status as a focal point of the world of wine."

Anton analysed the competition entries for eighteen years and took part in the judging of the wines & spirits as a panel chairman. Air Marshall Sir Humphrey Edwardes Jones, KCB, CBE, AFE, was one of the most loyal supporters of the IWSC. A very distinguished former Spitfire test pilot, he came to Anton for advice about the planting of vines on his property in Kent. Wine makes friends, and although Sir Humphrey did not plant his vineyard he stayed in touch, and in 1975 accepted the invitation to become Chairman of Club Oenologique Ltd., (later renamed The International Wine & Spirit Competition Ltd.). The Lord (Edward) Montague of Beaulieu became Hon President that same year, and each subsequent year a new personality was invited to preside over the IWSC. This practice continues to this day.
Highbury Harpers, the new owners of the IWSC, continue the quality asessment using the tried and tested formula, including chemical analysis.

After his retirement in 1988 Anton left for Spain and in 1992 he, his second wife Doris and a few other wine enthusiasts founded the Costa Blanca Wine Society. For ten years he organised monthly talks on wine with tastings for up to 150 CBWS members. Anton and Doris now live in Germany.

Part IV

Bibliography

Books on viticulture, wine making and wine appreciation.

This is an up-dated version of the list I had published in my book ´Applied Wine Chemistry and Technology´ (1969). Of course, such a list can never be complete and to limit its extent, I have listed only the titles that were published in English before 1990.
Many of the books are described in more detail by James M. Gabler in his book ´Wine into Words - A History and Bibliography of Books in the English Language´ (1985).

Author	Title	Date
Aaron, Jan	Wine Routes of America: the complete Travel Guide to Vineyards and Wineries	1989
Aaron, S. J.	Guide to Vintage Wine Prices: 1979-80	1979
Abbott, J. H. C.	British Wines	1979
Abel, Dominick	Guide to the Wines of the United States	1979
Abraham, Neville and Anne-Gale R.	The Wine Quiz Book	1979
Accum, Frederick Chr.	A Treatise on the Art of Making Wine from Native Fruits	1820
Ace, Donald and James Eakin	Wine Making as a Hobby	1977
Acton, Bryan .	Making Wines Like Those You Buy	1967
	Recipes for Prizewinning Wines	1971
Adams, John Festus	An Essay on Brewing, Vintage and Distillation etc.	1970
Adams, Leon D.	The Common Sense Book of Wine	1958
	How to Buy, Store Serve and Enjoy Wine	1964
	The Wines of America	1973
	Revitalizing the California Wine Industry	1974
Adams, Peter	The Wine Lover´s Quiz Book:Challenging	

	Questions and Answers for Wine Buffs and Bluffers	1987
Adams, Tate	Diary of a Vintage: The Workcycle of the Year 1979 at Wynns Coonawarra Estate in South Australia	1981
Adams, William H.	Confessions of a Lil' Ole Winemaker	1975
Adkins, Jan	The Craft of Making Wine	1971
Adlum, John	A Memoir on the Cultivation of the Vine in America and the best Mode of Making Wine	1823
	Adlum on Making Wines	1826
Aeuckens, Annely	Vinyeyard of the Empire: Ealy Barossa Vignerons	1988
Ainsworth, Jim	Red Wine Guide: A Complete Introductio to Choosing Red Wine	1990
	The Simon & Schuster Pocket Guide to Red Wines	1990
	The Simon & Schuster Pocket Guide to White Wines	1990
	White Wine Guide: A Complete Introduction to Choosing White Wine	1990

*

Akenhead, D.	Viticulture Research	1929
Allen, David Rayvern (Editor)	Arlott on Wine	1986
Allen, Eileen. Ed.	Wine and Cookery	1964
Allen H. Warner	Claret	1924
	Sherry	1924
	The Wines of France	1924
	Gentlemen, I Give You Wine	1930
	The Romance of Wine	1931
	Mr. Clerihew, Wine Merchant	1933
	Number Three St. James' Street: A History of Berry's the Wine Merchants	1950
	A Contemplation of Wine	1951
	Natural Red Wines	1951
	Sherry and Port	1952
	White Wines and Cognac	1952
	Through the Wine Glass	1954
	Good Wine from Portugal	1957
	A History of Wine: Great Vintage Wines	

	from Homeric Age to the present Day	1962
Allen, John Fisk	The Wines of Portugal	1963
	The Culture of the Grape	1847
	A Practical Treatise on the Culture and Treatment of the Grape Vine	1848
Allen, Michael	The Long Holiday - Wine in Provence	1974
Allen, Percy	Burgundy: The Splendid Duchy	1912
Alton, R. E. and Sam Aaron	The Pleasures of the Bottle	1966
Ambrosi, Dr. Hans	Comparison of Rootstocks in South Africa	1967
	Where the Great German Wines Grow	1979
	Wine Atlas and Dictionary - Germany	1976
Amerine, Maynard A.	Laboratory Procedures for Enology	1951
Amerine, Maynard A. and William Cruess	The Technology of Wine Making	1960
Amerine, Maynard A. and Maynard, Joslyn	Commercial Production of Table Wines	1941
	Commercial Production of Dessert Wines	1941
	Table Wines: The Technology of their Production in California	1970
Amerine, A. and C. S. Ough	Wine and Must Analysis	1974
	Methods for Analysis of Must and Wines	1980
Amerine, Maynard A., Harold W. Berg and William Cruess	Technology of Wine Making	1972
Amerine, Maynard A. and E. B. Roessler	Wines: Their Sensory Evaluation	1976
Amerine, Maynard A. and V. Singleton	Wine: An Introduction for Americans	1965
Amerine, Maynard A. and A.J.Winkler	Grape Varieties for Wine Production	1943
Ames, Richard	A Search after Claret	1691
	A Farther Search after Claret	1691
	The Bacchanalian Sessions, or Contemplation of Liquors	1693
Amis, Kingsley	Kingsley Amis on Drink	1973
Andersen, J. B.	A Basic Guide to Appreciating Wine	1979
Anderson, Burton	Vino: The Wines and Winemakers of Italy	1980
	Pocket Guide to Italian Wines	1982
Anderson, F. Stanley and Raymond Hull	The Art of Making Wine	1968
	The Advanced Winemaker's Practical Guide	

121

1975

Andrae, E. H.	A Guide to the Cultivation of the Grape Vine in Texas and Introductions for Wine-Making	1890
Andrews, S. W.	Be a Wine and Beer Judge	1977
Anstie, Francis E.	On the Uses of Wine in Health and Disease	1870
Antcliff, A. J.	Some Wine Grape Varieties for Australia	1976
	Major Wine Grape Varieties of Australia	1980
Antz, August	Legends of the Rhineland	1967
Appleyard, Alex	Make Your Own Wine	1953
Arlott, John	Krug: House of Champagne	1976
	Wine	1984
Arlott, John and Christopher Fielden	Burgundy, Vines and Wines	1978
Arnaldus, de Villanova	The Earliest Book on Wine, hand written	1310
	(first printed edition, in German)	1478
	(first Englich edition)	1943
Asbury, Herbert	The Great Illusion: An Informal History of Prohibition	1950
Ash, Douglas	How to Identify English Drinking Glasses and Decanters	1962
	How to Identify English Silver Drinking Vessels 600 - 1830	1964
Asher, Gerald	On Wine	1982
Aspler, Tony	Vintage Canada	1983
Austin, Cedric	The Science of Wine	1968
	The Good Wines of Europe	1972
	Wines and Wherefores of Winemaking	1973
Axler, Bruce H.	Practical Wine Knowledge	1974
Aye, John	The Humor of Drinking	1934
	Wine Wisdom	1934
Aylett, Mary	Country Wines	1953
	Encyclopaedia of Home-Made Wines	1957
Babo, Carl von	Reports on the Viticulture in the Cape Colony	1887
Bachchan, H.	The House of Wine	1950
Bagenall, B. W.	The Decendents of the Pioneer Winemakers of South Australia	1946
Bagnall, Gordon A.	Wines of South Africa	1961
Bailey, Liberty Hyde	American Grape Training	1893
Baker, John. Ed.	The Paragon of Wines and Spirits	1972

Baldwinson, John	Plonk and Super-Plonk	1977
Baker, Tony	Wolf Blass. A Journey in Wine	1991
Balzer, Robert L.	California's Best Wines	1948
	The Pleasures of Wine	1964
	Adventures in Wine	1969
	The Uncommon Heritage -	
	The Paul Masson Story	1970
	Book of Wines and Spirits	1973
	Wines of California	1978
	The Los Angeles Times Book of	
	California Wines	1984
Barrington-Brock, Ray	Outdoor Grapes in Cold Climates	
	(Report No. 1)	1949
	More Outdoor Grapes (Report No. 2)	1950
	Progress with Vines and Wines	
	(Report No. 3)	1961
	Starting a Vineyard (Report No. 4)	1964
Barron, A. F.	Vines and Vine Culture	1883
Barry, Sir Edward	Observations Historical and Medical on the	
	Wines of Ancients and the Analogy between	
	them and Modern Wines	1775
Barty-King, Hugh	A Tradition on English Wine	1977
Batchelor, Denzil	For What We are about to Receive	1964
	Wines Great and Small	1969
Batty, R. B.	The "medicated wines" Fraud as Denounced	
	by Doctors	1913
Baumann, C.M. and		
F.W.Michel	German Wine Alas and Vineyard Register	1977
Baus, Herbert S.	How to Wine Your Way to Good Health	1973
Bausch, Eric	The Luxembourg Moselle and its Wines	1986
Bayard, Luke	The Complete Wine Guide	1969
Beach, Frank Hainer	Grape Growing in Ohio	1944
Beadle, Leigh	Making Fine Wines and Liqueurs at Home	1971
Bear, J. W.	The Viticultural Resources of Victoria	
	(Australia)	1893
	The Fortification and Falsification of Wine	1895
Beardsall, Francis	Treatise on the Natural Properties and	
	Composition of Ancientand Modern Wines	
		1839
Beatty-Kingston, Will.	Claret: Its Production and Treatment	1895
Beaulieu, Francois	French Wine	1984
Beaune		1984
Beaven, Donald	Wines for Dining	1977

Beck, E. James	Wine: Its Culture and Making	1946
Beck, E, James. Ed.	The Aesthetics of Wine, the History of Wine in Australia	1946
Beck, Frederick K.	The Fred Beck Wine Book	1964
Beck, Hastings	Meet the Cape Wines	1955
Beckett, Richard	What is Wine That?	1975
Beckett, Richard and Donald Hogg	The Bulletin Book of Australian Wineries	1979
Beckwith, A. R.	The Vintner's Story	1959
Beckwith, Edward L.	Practical Notes on Wine	1868
Bedford, J. R.	Discovering English Vineyards	1982
Beech, Frederick W. and A. Pollard	Winemaking and Brewing	1972
	Wines and Juices	1961
Beach, F. W., E. Catlow and E. G. Gilbert	Growing Vi nes in the Open in Great Britain	1974
Beedell, Suzanne	Winemaking and Home Brewing	1969
Begin, Emile A. N. J.	Wine in Different Forms of Anaemia and Atonic Gout	1877
Belfrage, Nicholas	Life Beyond Lambrusco	1985
Bell, Bibiane	The Wine Book	1969
Belloc, Hilaire	Advice (on serving, bottling and drinking wines)	1960
Belows, Charles	Madeira	1900
Belperroud, John	The Vine: with instruction for its cultivation for a period of six years the treatment of the soil and how to make wine from Victorian Grapes	1859
Belth, George	Household Guide to Wines and Liquors	1934
Bennett, R.	Bennett's Guide to Winemaking	1852
Benson, Jeffrey and A. MacKenzie	Sauternes, A Study of the Great Sweet Wines of Bordeaux	1979
	The Wines of Saint-Emilion and Pomerol	1983
Benson, Robert	Great Winemakers of California	1977
Bentley, Iris	Wine with a Merry Heart	1959
Benwell, W. S.	Coonawarra, a Vignoble	1973
	Journey to Wine in Victoria	1960
Berg, Harold W.	Grape Classification by Total Acidity	1960
Bergeron, Victor Jules	My Selection of California Wines	1966
Beridze, G.	Wines and Cognacs of Georgia	1965

Berkmann, Joseph
and Allen Hall   Berkmann and Hall's Good Wine Guide   1978
Bernstein, Leonard S. The Official Guide to Wine Snobbery   1982
Berry, Charles Walter Viniana   1929
                      Miscellany of Wine   1932
                      In Search of Wine   1935
Berry, Cyril John J. First Steps in Winemaking   1963
                      Amateur Winemaker Recipes   1968
Berry-Smith, F.   Vines Under Glass   1962
                      Viticulture   1973
Bespaloff, Alexis   The First Book of Wine   1971
                      The Signet Book of Wine   1971
                      The Family Circle Guide to Wine   1973
                      Guide to Expensive Wines   1973
                      The Fireside Book of Wine   1977
Bewerunge, Wilhelm German Wine on the Danube and Rhine   1935
Biane, Philo   Wine Making in Southern California and
                      Recollections of Fruit Industries   1972
Bickerton, L. M.   An Illustrated Guide to Eighteenth-Century
                      English Drinking Glasses   1971
Biddle, Anthony J. D. The Land of Wine - Madeira   1901
                      Red Wine in South Africa   1971
Bijur, George   Wines with long Noses   1951
Billington, Ernest The Handicap of the Wine Trade   1934
Bioletti, Frederick T. Bench Grafting Resistant Vines   1900
                      Resistant Vineyards: Grafting, Planting,
                      Cultivation   1906
Bird, William   French Wines: A Practical Guide for Cellar-
                      men, Wine-Butlers and Connoisseurs   1955
Birmingham, F. A.   Esquire Drink Book   1956
Bishop, Allen   Knowing and Selling Wines, Liquors,
                      Liqueurs and Cordials   1934
Bishop, Geoffrey C.   Australian Winemaking:
                      The Roseworthy Influence   1980
                      The Vineyards of Adelaide   1977
Bleasdale, J. Ignatius An Essay on the Wines Sent to the Inter-
                      colonial Exibition by the Colonies of
                      Victoria, New South Wales and South
                      Australia, with Critical Remarks on the
                      Present Condition and the Prospects of the
                      Wine Industry in Australia   1876
                      On Colonial Wines: A Paper Before the
                      Royal Society of Victoria, 13th May 1867 1867

	Pure Native Wine Considered as an Article	
	of Food and Luxury	1868
Blout, Jessy Schilling	A brief Economic History of the California	
	Wine Growing Industry	1943
Blum, Howard L.	The Wines and Vines of Europe	1974
Blumberg, Robert S.		
and Hannun, H.	California Wine	1973
	The Fine Wines of California	1973
Boake, W. B.	The Production of Wine in Australia	1889
Bode, Charles	Wines of Italy	1956
Bodington, C.	Wines of the Bibel	1887
Boehm, E. W.		
and Tulloch, H. W.	Great of South Australia	1967
Boireau, Raimond	Wines, their Care and Treatment in Cellar	
	and Store	1889
Bollito, Hector	The Wine of the Douro	1956
Bolsmann, Eric	Bertram's Guide to South African Wines	
	of Origin	1977
	The South African Wine Dictionary	1977
Bone, Arthur	"How to" Book of Chosing and Enjoying	
	Wine	1981
Bonetti, Edward	The Wine Cellar	1977
Bonnard, H. D.	The Bordeaux International Exibition of	
	Wines	1984
Booth, David	The Art of Wine-making in all its Branches	
		1834
Borg, P.	Report on a Tour of Inspection in the Wine-	
	growing Districts of Western Europe and	
	Algeria	1922
Born, Wina	The Concise Atlas of Wines	1974
Bosdari, C. de	Wines of the Cape	1955
Boswell, Peyton	Winemakers Manual	1935
Boushe, Paul	Wine, its Connection with Health	1913
Boulestin, X. M.	What Shall We Have to Drink?	1933
Bourke, Arthur	Winecraft; The Encyclopaedia of Wines	
	and Spirits	1935
Bracony, Frank	The U.S. Wine Market	1977
Bradford, Sarah	The Englishman's Wine: The Story of Port	1969
Bradley, Nellie H.	Wine as a Medicine	1873
Bradley, Richard	The Vineyard	1724
Bradley, Robin	Three Days of Wine	1977
	Australian Wine Pocket Book	1978
Bradt, O. A.	The Great Ontario	1972

126

Bragato, Romeo	Report on the Prospects of Viticulture in	
	New Zealand	1895
	Viticulture in New Zealand	1906
Brannt, William T.	A Practical Treatise on the Manufacture of	
	Cider and Fruit Wines	1914
Bravery, H. E.	Sucessful Modern Winemaking	1961
	Sucessful Winemaking at Home	1962
	Amateur Winemaking	1964
	The Complete Book of Winemaking	1971
	Home Wine-Making and Vine Growing	1973
	Home-made Wines and Liqueurs	1974
	Home Wine and Beer Making	1974
	Country Wines and Cordials	1980
Bredenbek, Magnus	What Shall We Drink?	1934
Breman, Paul	The Pinguin Guide to Cheaper Wines	1976
Brenner, Gary	The Naked Grape	1975
Bright, William	Bright's Single Stem, Dwarf and Renewel	
	System.....	1860
Brink, André P.	Dessert Wine in South Africa	
Broadbent, Michael	Wine Tasting	1968
	The Complete Guide to Wine Tasting	1984
	The Great Vintage Wine Book	1980
	Guidance to the Technique of Tasting	1963
	Michael Broadbent's Complete Guide to	
	Wine Tasting and Wine Cellars	1984
Broadbent, Michael	Christie's Vintage Wine Price Index	1982
(Ed).	Christie's Wine Review (9 vols.) 1972 - 1980	
Brook, Stephen	Liquid Gold -Dessert Wines of the World	1987
Brown, Cora	The Wine Cook Book...	1934
	The Wining and Dining Quiz	1939
Brown, Michael		
and Cybil	Food and Wine of South-West France	1980
Brown, Sanborn C.	Wines and Beers of Old New England	1978
Browne, Charles	The Gun Club Drink Book	1979
Buchanan, Robert	The Culture of the Grape and Wine Making	
		1850
Buck, John	Take A Little Wine	1969
Buckley, Francis	A History of Old English Glass	1925
Burden, Rosemary	Wines and Wineries of Southern Vales	1976
	A Family in Fine Winemaking;	
	125 Years of Hardy and Sons; 1853-1978	1978
Burger, Robert E.	The Jug Wine Book	1980
Burgess, H. T.	The Fruit of the Vine	1878

Burka, Fred
and Massee, William Pulling Corks   1951
Burman, José   Wine of Constantia   1979
Burroughs, David
  and Norman Bezzant The New Wine Companion   1975
                    The Wine Trade Student's Companion   1975
                    Wine Regions of the World   1979
Burt, Jocelyn   Wineries of the Barossa Valley   1975
Busby, James   A Treatise on the Culture of the Vine and
                      the Art of Winemaking   1825
                    A Manual of Plain Directions for Planting
                      and Cultivating Vineyards and for Making
                      Wine in New South Wales   1830
                    Journal of a Tour through some of the
                      Vineyards of Spain and France   1833
                    The Australian Landowner's Guide to Wine
                      in New South Wales   1843
Bush, Isidore   Illus. Desciptive Catalouge of Grape Vines
                                                                1869
Bush, John H.   Veritas in Vino   1973
Busselle, MichaelThe Wine Lovers Guide to France   1986
Butler, Frank Hedges Wine Lands of the World   1926
Butler, Ormon Rourke Observations on the California Vine
                      Disease   1910
Butler, Robin and
  Gillian Walkling The Book of Wine Antiques   1987
Bynum, Lindley   California Wines: How to Enjoy Them   1955
Caine, Philip J.   The Wonderful World of Wine   1976
Caldaway, Jeffrey   Wine-Tour: Napa Valley   1979
                    Wine-Tour: Sonoma-Mendocino   1979
Calpin, G. H.   Sherry in South Africa   1978
Cambiaire, Celestin P.The Black Horse of the Apocalypse   ;
                      Wine, Alcohol and Civilization   1932
Campbell, George W. Desciptive List of Hardy Native Grape
                      Vines   1870
Campbell, Ian M.   Remenisences of a Vintner   1950
                    Wayward Tendrils of the Vine   1947
Caradeuc, H. de   Grape Culture and Winemaking in the
                      South   1859
Carey, Mary   Step-by-step Winemaking   1973
Carling, Thomas E. Wine Etiquette   1949
                    Wine-Wise. How to Know, Choose and
                      Serve Wine   1949

	The Complete Book of Drink	1951
	Wine Lore; A Critical Analysis of Wine Dogma	1954
	Wine Aristocracy; A Guide to the Best Wines of the World	1957
	Wine Data	1959
	Wine Drinker's Aide-Memoire	1959
	Wine. Thumbnail Sketches of Wines of the World	1960

Carlisle, D. T.
and Elizabeth Dunn Wining and Dining with Rhyme and
                                   Reason 1933
Carnell, Philip Pery A Treatise on Family Wine Making 1814
Carosso, Vincent P. The California Wine Industry, 1830-1895:
                                   A Study of the Formative Years 1951
Carr, John Geoffrey Biological Principles in Fermentation 1958
                                   Aroma and Flavour in Winemaking 1974
Carre, G. F. Drinking in France 1974
Carrier, R. Food, Wine and Friends 1980
Carter, Everett Wine and Poetry 1976
Carter, Youngman Drinking Bordeaux 1966
                                   Drinking Burgundy 1966
                                   Drinking Champagne and Brandy 1968
Carvalho, Bento de
and Lopez Correia The Wine Portugal 1979
Casanave, Armand Practical Manual of the Vine in tne Gironde
                                        1885
Casas, Penelope Food and Wine of Spain 1984
Cassagnac, Paul de French Wines 1930
Castella, François de Home Wine Making 1921
                                   The Grapes of South Australia 1942
Castella, Hubert de John Bull's Vineyard 1886
                                   Hand Book on Viticulture for Victoria 1891
Castillo, José Del
and Hallet David R. The Wines of Spain 1972
Cattell, Hudson
and Stauffer L. Miller Pennsylvania Wines 1976
                                   The Wines of the East, the Hybrids 1978
                                   The Wines of the East, the Vinifera 1979
                                   The Wines of the East, Native American Grapes 1980
Cavanagh, John &
Frederick F. Clairmonte

	Alcoholic Beverages: Dimensions of Corporate Power	1985
Cave, Peter L.	Best Drinking Jokes	1973
Cazubon, D.	Treatise and Practical Guide of the Apparatus for the Fabrication of Gaseous Drinks, Sparkling Wines, etc.	1876
Cerletti, G. B.	Desciptive Account on the Wine Industry of Italy	1888
Challoner, F.	Port, Oporto and Portugal	1913
Chaloner, Len	What the Vintners Sell	1926
Chamberlain, Bern. P.	A Treatise on the Making of Palatable Table Wines....	1931
Chappaz, George and A. Henriot	The Champagne Vine Country and Champagne Wine	1920
Chaptal, Jean A. C.	Treatise upon Wines	1823
Chase, Emily	The Pleasures of Cooking with Wine	1967
Chatterton, B. A.	Home Wine-Making	1972
	Sunday Mail Guide to South Australian Wineries	1973
Chene, P. le	Helpful hints for Sommerliers and Wine Waiters	1973
Chidgey, Graham	Guide to the Wines of Burgundy	1977
Chimay, Jacqueline de	The Life and Time of Madame Veuve Cliquot Ponsardin	1961
Chirich, Nancy	Life With Wine	1984
Chlebnikowski, Nick	European Wine Vintages	1981
Chowdowski, A. T.	Wine, its use and Ubuse: The Fermented Wines of the Bibel	1893
Chorlton, William	The American Grape Grower's Guide	1852
Christ, Edwin and J. R. Fisk	That Book About Wine	1955
Christodoulou, Dimit.	The Evolution of Rural Land use Pattern in Cyprus	1959
Chroman, Nathan	The Treasury of American Wines	1973
Church, Ruth Ellen	The American Guide to Wines	1963
	Entertaining with Wine	1976
Churchill, Creighton	A Notebook for the Wines of France	1961
	The World of Wines	1964
	The Great Wine Rivers	1971
Chute, Chaloner W.	A History of the Vyne in Hampshire	1888
Claire, Aileen	The Connoisseur's Wine Book	1973

Clark, Selden   California's Wine Industry and its Financing
                                                                1941
Clarke, Ebeneezer   The Worship of Bacchus: a Great delusion 1877
Clarke, Frank K.   Make Your Wine at Home; A Book for
                        Beginners   1968
Clarke, Nick   Bluff Your Way in Wine   1967
                        The Bluffer's Guide to Wine   1971
Clarke, William   Complete Cellar Manual   1829
Cleland, Charles   Abstracts of the Several Laws that are now
                        in Force, Relating to the Importation and
                        Exportation on Wines. Into and Out of
                        Great Britain   1737
Cleland, Robert G.   California in our Time (1900-1940)   1947
Clueslant, F.   Disease of the Vine and how to Cure It 1886
Coates, Clive   Claret   1982
Cobb, Gerald   Oporto Older and Newer   1966
Cockburn, Ernest H.   Port Wine and Oporto   1950
Cockburn, F. A.   Wine and The Wine Trade   1947
Cocks, Charles
 and E. Feret   Bordeaux and Its Wines   1883
Codman, Charles R. S. Years and Years; Some Vintage Years in
                        French Wines   1935
                        Vintage Dinners   1937
Codman, Mrs.Theodore
Laroque   Was it a Holiday? (Burgundy, Anjou and
                        Bordeaux)   1935
Colbridge, A.M.   Wine Making   1973
Colburn, Frona Eunice Wines and Vines of California; A Treatise
                        on the Ethics of Wine-Drinking (1889) 1973
Colburn, Frona E. W. In Old Vintage Days   1937
Cole, Emma Aubert   Champagne at the Wedding   1947
Cole, R.L.   Sacramental Wine: Intoxicating, or non-
                        Intoxicating ?   1913
Collier, Carole   505 Wine Questions Your Friends Can´t
                        Answer   1983
Columella, Lucius
 Junius Moderatus   On Agriculture (De Agricultura ca. 65 A.D.)
                        English Translation   1941
Combe, William   A History of Madeira   1821
Conant, James B. Ed. Pasteur´s Study of Fermantation   1952
Conn, Donald   D. The California Vineyard Industry   1932
Cook, Fred S.   The Wine and Wineries of California   1966
Cook, Philip   A Wine Merchants' Assessment Of

	Burgundy	1965
Cooke, Matthew	Injurious Insect of the Orchard, Vineyards...	
		1883
Cool, R. C.	The Scuppernong Grape: Its Growth and Care under Vineyard Conditions	1913
Combe, Brian G.	Phylloxera and its Relation to South Australian Viticulture	1963
Cooper, Derek	The Beverage Report	1970
	Wine With Food	1980
Cooper, John Ralph and Vaile, J. E.	Response of American Grapes to Various Treatments and Vineyard Practices	1939
Cooper, Michael	The Wines and Vineyards of New Zealand	1984
Cooper, Rosalind	The Wine Book	1982
	The Wine Almanac	1986
Cossart, Noel	Madeira The Island Vineyard	1984
Couche, Donald D.	Modern Detection and Treatment of Wine Diseases and Defects	1935
Courtney, J. M. de	The Culture of the Vine and Emigration	1863
	The Canada Vine Grower	1866
Couveslant, F.	Disease of The Wine and How to Cure It	1886
Cover, Doe. Ed	The Price Guide to Good Wine	1883
Cox, Harry	The Wines of Australia	1967
Coxen, C.	Vine Disease	1848
Crabtree, Bill	The Best Wine Recipes	1979
Cradock, John	An ABC of Wine Drinking	1954
	Wining and Dining in France with Bon Viveur	1959
Cradock, Johnnie	Wine for Today	1975
Craig, Elizabeth	Wine in the Kitchen	1934
Crawford, Anne	A History of the Vintners' Company	1977
Crawford, Iain	Wine on a Budget	1964
	Make Me a Wine Connoisseur	1969
Critchfield, Burke H., Carl F. Wente and A. G. Frericks	The California Wine Industry During the Depression	1972
Croft, John	A Tretease on the Wines of Portugal...	1787
Croft-Cooke, Rupert	Sherry	1955
	Port	1956
	Madeira	1961
	Wine and Other Drinks	1962

Crosby, Everett   The Vintage Years;
                      the Story of High Tor Vinyards   1973
Crosland, J.   Crosland's Wine Calculator...   1881
Cross, Frank Baker   Grapes in Oklahoma   1939
Crotch, W. W. Ed.   The Complete Year Book of French Quality
                      Wines, Spirits and Liqueurs   1947
Croze, Austin de   What to Eat and Drink in France   1931
Cruess, William Vere The Principles and Practice of Wine Making
                                                              1934
                      Investigation of the Flor Sherry Process 1948
                      A Half Century of Food and Wine
                      Technology   1967
Cruess, William Vere,
  Maynard A. Joslyn
  and L. G. Saywell   Laboratory Examination of Wine and
                      Fermented Fruit Products   1934
Csavas, Zoltan   The Louis Martini Winery St. Helena   1983
Cunynghame, Francis Reminiscenses of an Epicure   1955
Cuthill, James   A Treatise on the Vine Disease   1873
Dali, Salvadore   The Wines of Gala - Over a Hundred
                      Illustrations by Dali with Texts by Louis Orizet
                                                              1978
Dallas, Philip   The Great Wines of Italy   1974
                      Italian Wines   1974
                      Italian Wines   1974
Daraio, John P.   Healthful and Therapeutic Properties
                      of Wine...   1937
D'armand, F.   Art of Fine Wine Drinking   1903
David, Elizabeth   An Omelette and a Glass of Wine   1985
David, H. J. Ed.   The Wine Book of South Africa. The Western
                      Province of the Cape and Its Wine Industry
                                                              1936
Davidson, William M.The Great Phylloxera in California   1921
Davidson, William R. The Wholesale Wine Trade in Ohio.
                      Covers the period 1934-54   1954
Davis, Derek C.   English Bottles and Decanters 1650-1900 1972
Davis, J. Irving   A Beginners' Guide to Wines and Spirits 1934
Davis, Pat (ed)   Oysters and Champagne   1986
Davis, S. F.   History of the Wine Trade   1969
De Bernardi Mateos, P.Wines from the District of Utiel-Requena
                      (Spain)   1970
De Blij, Harm J. Wine, A Geographic Appreciation   1983
De Groot, Roy AndriesThe Wines of California, the Pacific North-

133

	west and New York	1982
De Jongh, S. J.	Encyclopaedia of South African Wine	1976
Debuigne, Gerard	Larousse Dictionary of Wines of the World	
		1976
DeChambeau, André	Creative Winemaking	1972
Deighton, Len. Ed.	Drinksmanship. Town's Album of Fine	
	Wines and Spirit	1964
Delaforce, John	The Factory House of Oporto	1979
Delmon, Philip	Making Wine Once a Week	1971
	Ten Types of Table Wine	1971

Delmon, Philip
  and B. C. A. Turner Quick and Easy Winemaking from
                       Concentrates and Fruit Juices   1973
Denman, L.   A Brief Discussion on Wine...   1861
                     Denman's Annual Wine Report   1862
                     The Vine and Its Fruit   1864
                     Wine as It is Drunk in England...   1865
                     Wine, the Advantages of Pure and Natural
                     Wine...   1865
                     Wine as It Should Be...   1866
                     Wine and Its Adulterations   1867
                     What Should We Drink   1868
                     Pure Wine and How to Know It   1869
                     What is Wine?   1874
                     Wine and Its Counterfeits   1876
Denny, Ronald C.   The Trueth about Breath Tests   1970
Dennis, C.B.   A Background to Mead Making   1961
Denniston, G.   Grape Culture in Steuben County in
                     New York   1865
Despeissis, J. A. The Vineyard And the Cellar   1894
Dettori, R. G.   Italian Wines and Liqueurs   1953
Dewey, Suzette   Wine for Those Who have Forgotten and
                     Those Who Want to Know   1934
Dexter, Philip   Notes on French Wines   1933
Dickens, Cedric Drinking with Dickens   1980
Digiacomo, Louis J. The Clear and Simple Wine Guide   1981
Dill, George H.   Prohibition and the Vineyard   1906
Dingman, Stanley T. The Wine Cellar and Journal Book   1972
Director, Anne   The Standard Wine Cook Book   1948
Disher, M. Willson   Winkels and Champagne   1938
Dix, Irving W.
  and Magnus J. R.   American Grape Varieties   1937
Don, Robin   Off the Shelf   1967

	Wine	1968
Donna, Gail		
and Lucy Waverman	The Pennypincher's Wine Guide	1974
Dornat, C. C.	The Wine and Spirit Merchant's Own Book; a Manual for the Manufacturer, and a Guide for the Dealer in Wines, Spirits...	1855
Dorozynski, Alexander		
and Bibiane Bell	The Wine Book	1969
Doughty, Brian. Ed	A Guide to Good Wine	1970
Dovaz, Michael	Encylopaedia of the Great Wines of Bordeaux	1981
Dowley, D. M.	Nuttall's Wine Facts	1979
Downey, A. J.	Australian Grape Grower's Manual for the Use of Beginners	1895
Doxat, John. Ed.	The Indespensible Drinks Book (With a section by Jancis Robinson)	1981
Drake, Albert	Wine and You	1970
Drinkwater, Caleb	How to Serve Wine and Beer	1933
Driscoll, W. P.	The Beginnings of the Wine Industry in the Hunter Valley	1969
Driver, John	Letters from Medeira	1836
Driver, Sydney C.	Some Principles of the Wine Trade	1909
Druitt, Robert M. D.	Reports on Cheap Wines of France, Italy, Austria, Greece and Hungary...	1865
Du Breuil, Alphonse	Vineyard Culture Improved and Cheapened	1867
Du Breuil, M.	The Thomery System of Grape Culture	1876
Du Plessis, C. S.	A Study of Wine Bouquet Precursors in Grapes	1970
Du Plessis, Stefanus J.	Anthracnose of Vines and its Controls in South Africa	1940
	Bacterial Blight of Vines (Vlamsiekte) in South Africa Caused by Erwinia Vitivora	1940
	Comparison of the Effectiveness of Various Fungicides	1939
Dubois, Raymond	Trenching and Subsoiling for American Vines	1901
Dubois, Raymond		
and P. W. Wilkenson	New Methods of Grafting and Budding as Applied to Reconstitution with American Vines	1901
Dufour, John James	The American Vine-Dresser's Guide	1826
Duijker, Hubrecht	The Great Wines of Burgundy	1977

	Book of Wines	1974
	Australian Complete Book of Wine	1976
	Complete Book of Australian Wine	1985
Evans, Lloyd	Wine	1973
Evans, Tom	The Compleat Wine-Maker	1970
Fabre, Jean H.C.	Analysis of Wines and Interpretations of Analytical Results	1945
Fadiman, Clifton. Ed.	Dionysus: A Case of Vintage Tales about Wine	1962
Fadiman, Clifton and Sam Aaron	Wine Buyers Guide	1977
	The Joys of Wine	1975
Faith, Nicholas	The Winemasters	1978
	Chateau Margaux	1982
	Victorian Vineyard: Chateau Loudenne and Gilbeys	1983
Fallon, James Thomas	Handbook of Australian Vines and Wines	1874
	Murray Valley Vineyard	1874
	The Wines of Australia	1876
Flaludy, Andrew	The Crisis in the Languedoc Wine Trade	1977
Farer, Winton	Wine Making at Home	1973
Faubel, Arthur Louis	Cork and the American Cork Industry	1941
Fauqueux, M.C.	The Men who Make Wine	1955
Fegan, Patrick W.	Vineyards and Wineries of America	1982
Feldman, Herman	Prohibition: Its Economic and Industrial Aspects	1927
Fenton, Ferrar	The Bible and Wine	1938
Feret, Edouard	Bordeaux and Its Wines Classed by order of Merit	1899
Fessler, Julius H.	The Art of Making Wine and Wine Vinegar	1941
Feuerheerd, H.L.	The Gentleman's Cellar and Butler's Guide	1899
Field, S.S.	The American Drink Book	1953
Fielden, Christopher	White Burgundy	1988
Finley, A.K.	The Phylloxera - A short Treatise on the Vine Destroyer	1880
Firth, James Francis	The Cooper's Company	1848
Fisher, Mary F.K.	The Story of Wine in California	1962
Fisher, S.I.	Obesrvations on the Character and Culture of the European Vine	1834
Fletcher, Wyndham	Port: An Introduction to Its History and Delights	1978

Flower, Raymond	Chianti: The Land, the People and the Wine	
		1979
Flucher, Henri André	Wines	1973
Foex, G.	Manual of Modern Viticulture:	
	Reconstruction with American Vines	1902
Fonseca, A.M. de	Port Wine. Notes on its History, Production	
	and Technology	1981
Foote, E.J.	Will You take Wine	1935
Forbes, Ellert	Wines for Everyman	1937
Forbes, Patrick	Champagne: The Wine, the Land and the	
	People	1967
	The Story of Maison Moet et Chandon	1972
Ford, Gene	The ABC of Wine, Brew and Spirits	1980
	Gen Forbes Illustrated Guide to Wines,	
	Beers and Spirits	1983
Forest, Louis	Wine Album, Adapted from:	
	Monseigneur Le Vin, Paris 1927	1982
Fornachon, J. C. M.	Bacterial Spoilage in Fortified Wines	1943
	Studies of the Sherry Flor	1952
	A Textbook for the Australian Sherry Maker	
		1972
Forrest, Joseph James	Curious Reflections on the use made of	
	Elederberry Wine, which is now grown in	
	the Wine Dostrict of Alto Douro	1845
	An Illustrated Paper on the Vine Disease	
	in the Districts of the Alto Douro	1854
	Observtions on Port Wine: Together with	
	Documents Proving the Existence of these	
	Abuses, and Letters on the same Subject...	
	Published in his own Defence	1845
	Port and Wine in Portugal	1845
	Short Treatise on the Chemical Changes	
	which often take place in Port-Wines Stored	
	in England	1858
Foster, Alfred	Through the Wine List	1924
Foster, William	A Short History of the Cooper´Company	1944
Fougner, G.Selmer	Along the Wine Trail (5 vols)	1934 - 1937
Francis, Alan David	The Wine Trade	1972
Francis, L.R.	100 Years of Wine Making 1865-1965	1966
Franz, Arnulf	The New Wine Book	c1934
Fredericksen, Paul	The Authentic Haraszthy Story	1947
Frumkin, L.	The Science and Technique of Wine	1974
Funk, Wilfried John	If You Drink	1940

Gabler, James M.	Wine into Words. A History and Bibligraphy of Wine Books in the English Language	1985
Gabler, James M. and Joann Gabler	Wines of the Fouding Fathers	1976
Gale, R.	The Marketing of Wine and Vines in Australia	1970
Galet, Pierre	A Practical Ampelography: Grape Vine Identification	1978
Gallo, Ernest and Gallo Julio	Gallo Vineyards	1967
Gardner, John ed.	The Brewer, Distiller and Wine Manufacturer	1883
Garrett, Paul	The Art of Serving Wine	1905
Garvin, Fernende	French Wines	1968
Gayon, Ulysse	Studies on Wine-Sterilizing Machines	1901
Geiss, Lisbet	The Gay Language of Wine	1981
George, J. and B.Anderson	Easy Wine Making	1976
George, Rosemary	The Wines of Chablis and the Yonne	1984
Gibbons, Henry	The Wine Culture in California	1867
Gillette, Paul	Enjoying Wine	1976
Gillette, Peter and Paul Gillette	Playboy´s Book of Wine	1974
Ginestet	The Wines of France: Margeaux	1985
	The Wines of France: Saint Emilion	1985
Giordano, Frank	Texas Wines and Wineries	1984
Goff, Michael	Food and Wine	1972
Gohdes, Clarence, L.F.	Scuppernong, North Carolina´s Grape and its Wines	1982
Gold, Alex. Ed.	Wines and Spirits of the World	1968
Golding, Louis and André L. Simon	We Shall Eat and Drink Again	1941
Gonzalez Gordon, Manuel M.	Sherry: The Noble Wine	1972
Gore-Browne, Margaret	Let's Plant a Vineyard	1967
Gorman, Robert	Gorman on California Premium Wines	1975
Goswell, R.W.	Fortified Wines (Port and Sherry)	1966
Gould, Francis L.	Charles Krug Winery 1861-1961	1961
	Bottles and Bins	1965
	My Life with Wine (signed copy)	1972
Grace, Virginia R.	Amphoras and the Ancient Wine Trade of Athens	1969
Grazzi-Soncini, G.	Wine: Classification, Wine Tasting,	

139

	Qualirties and Defects	1892
Greg, Thomas Tylston	Through the Glass Lightly	1897
Gregor, Max	Notes upon Pure and Natural Wines of	
	Hungary	1869
Grohusko, Jacob A.	Jack´s Manual on the Vintage and Production,	
	Care and Handling of Wines, Liquors.....	1933
Grossmann, Harold J.	Imported Wines and Spirits	1961
	Grossman's Guide to Wines, Spirits and	
	Beers	1977
Grover, Linda	Napa Valley	1980
Guest, Cathrin	Winemakig	1979
Gunn, John and		
R. McK Gollan	Report onthe Wine Industry of Australia	1931
Gunn, Peter	Burgundy: Lanscape with Figures	1976
Gunyon, R. E.	The Wines of Central- and South-Eastern	
	Europe	1972
Guthrie, William	Remarks on Claret, Burgundy Champagne.	
	Their Dietic and Restorative uses.....	1889
Guyot, Jules	Culture of the Vine and Wine Making	1865
	Growth of the Vine and Principles of	
	Winemaking	1896
Gwynn, Stephen L.	Burgundy	1930
Gyori, Paul	The Fine Wines of Germay and all the	
	World´s Wine Lore	1965
Haarlem, J.R.	Variety Tests for Grapes for Wine	1954
Haggard, H.W. and		
E.M.Jellinek	Alcohol Explained	1942
Hahn, Dr..	Report on some Questions Connected with	
	Viticulture at the Cape	1882
Halász, Z.	Hungarian Wines through the Ages	1962
	The Book of Hungarian Wines	1981
Hall, James and		
John Bunton	Wines	1961
Hallgarten Peter	Chateauneuf- du- Pape	1961
	Cotes-du-Rhone. The Vineyards and	
	Villages of the Rhone Valley	1965
	The Problem of Acidity in White Wines	1966
	Guide to the Wines of the Rhone	1979
Hallgarten, S. F.	Rhineland Wineland	1951
	Alsace and its Wine Gardens	1957
	A Guide to Vineyards, Estates and Wines	
	of Germany	1974
	German Wines	1976

	Wine Scandal	\1976
	Alsace, its Wine Gardens, Cellars and Cuisine	1978
	The Wines and Wine Gardens of Austria	1979
Halliday, James	Wines and Wineries of New South Wales	1980
	Wines and Wineries of South Australia	1981
	Wines and Wineries of Western Australia	1982
	Wines and Wineries of Victoria	1982
	Coonawarra, the History, the Vignerons and the Wines	1983
	The Australian Wine Compendium	1985
Halliday, James and Ray Jarratt	The Wines and History of the Hunter Valley	1979
Hammond, H.	Notes on Wine and Vine Culture in France	1856
Hanckel, Norman	Australian and New Zealand Complete Book of Wine	1973
Hann, George E.	Some Notes on the Technical Study and Handling of Wines	1948
Hansen, Emil	Practical Studies in Fermentation	1896
Hansen, Jens	Wine and the Bible	1955
Hanson, Anthony	Burgundy	1982
Haraszthy, Agoston	Grape Culture, Wines and Wine-Making	1862
Haraszthy, Arpad	The Haraszthy Family	1866
	California Grapes and Wines	1883
Hardman, William	The Wine-Grower's and Wine Cooper's Manual	1877
Hardwick, Homer	Winemaking at Home	1954
Hardy, Thomas	Notes on the Vineyards of America and Europe	1885
	A Vigneron Abroad; Trip to South Africa	1899
Thomas K. Hardy	The Australian Wine Pictorial Atlas	1997
Harris, Mollie	Drop o'Wine	1983
Harrison, Brian	Drink and the Victorians	1971
Harris, Godfrey	Bristol Cream (Harvey's of Bristol Sherry)	1955
Harley, Joseph	The Wholesale and Retail Wine and Spirit Merchant's Companion and Complete Instructor to the Trade	1835
Hartmann, Dennis	Wines and Liqueurs, What and When, How to Serve them	1933
Hartshorne, Albert	Old English Glasses	1897
Haslegrove, C.P.	About Vines and Wines	1956

Haskell, Steve and Bruce Fingerhut	Read that Label: How to Tell What's Inside a Wine Bottle from What's on the Outside	1983
Hasler, G.E.	Wine Service in the Restaurant	1967
Hasler, Hall R.J.	Wine-Art Recipe Booklet	1977
Haszonics, Joseph and Stuart Barratt	Wine Merchandising	1963
Hatch, Evelyn M.	Burgundy Past and Present	1927
Hatch, Ted	The Anerican Wine Cookbook	1941
Hawker, Charlotte	Wine and Wine Merchants	1909
	Chats About Wine	
Hazan, Victor	Italian Wine	1982
	Hazelton, Nika Standen American Wines	1976
Healy, Maurice	Claret and the White Wines of Bordeaux	1934
	Stay me with Flagons	1949
Heath, Ambrose	Good Drinks	1939
	Home-Made Wines and Liqueurs	1961
Heaton, Nell St. John	Wines, Mixed Drinks and Savouries	1962
Heaton, Nell and André L. Simon	A Calendar of Food and Wine	1949
Heaton, Vernon	Choose a Wine and Cheese Party	1969
Herbert, Malcom R.	The Wine Lover's Cook Book	1984
Heckmann, Manfred	Corksrews	1981
Heddle, Enid Moodie	Story of a Vineyard: Chateau Tahbilk	1960
Hedrick, Ulysses P	The Grapes of New York	1908
	Manual of Amrican Grape Growing	1919
	Grapes and Wines from Home Vineyards	1945
Heide, Ralph Auf Der.	The Illustrated Wine Making Book	1973
Hellmann, R.	Food and Wine in Europe	1970
Henderson, Alexander	The History of Ancient and Modern Wines	1824
Henriques, E. Frank	The Signet Encyclopedia of Wine	1975
Hensche, C.A.	Obesrvations of Winemaking in Europe in Relation to the Winse Industry in Australia	1970
Henshaw, Dennis	Brush Your Teath with Wine	1960
Herbemont, N.A. A	Treatise on the Culture of the Vine and on Wine Making in the United States	1833
Herod, William P.	An Itroduction to Wines	1936
Herstein, Karl M. and Thomas Gregory	Chemistry and Technolgy of Wines and Liquors	1935

Heuckmann, Wilhelm The Grafted Vine; European Scions;
                    American Stocks; the End of Phylloxera 1964
Hewett, Edward and
  W.F. Axton   Convivial Dickens: The Drinks of Dickens
                      and His Friends   1983
Hewitson, Don   Enjoying Wine   1985
Hewitt, John TheodoreChemistruy of Winemaking: A report on
                      Oenological Research   1928
Hitchens, Phoebe   Wineman's Bluff   1973
Hightower, Penny   Cocktails with Wine   1977
Hilgard, Eugene W.   The Phylloxera or Grape Vine Louse, and
                      the Remedies for its ravages   1875
                      Report on Experiments on Fermenting Red
                      Wines and Related Subjects During the
                      Years 1886-7   1888
Hillman, Howard   The Diner's Guide to Wines   1978
Hines, Philip R.   The Wines and Wineries of Ohio   1973
Hinkle, Richard Paul Central Coast Wine Book   1980
                      Napa Valley Wine Book   1979
Hinton L.   Redman Wine; The Story of a Winemaker 1971
Hirschfeld, Albert M. The Standard Handbook on Wines and
                      Liquors   1907
Hocker, E.Curtis Hocker's Alcholic Beverage Encyclopedia 1941
Hocking, Anthony   Wine: Pride of South Africa   1973
Hofer, A.F.   Grape Growing in the Upper Rhine Valley 1878
Hogg, Anthony   Wine Mine: A First Anthology   1970
                      Off The Shelf   1972
                      Guide to Visiting Vineyard   1977
                      The Winetatser's Guide to Europe   1980
Holden, E.A.   The History of Viticulture and Wine Making
                      in Australia   1935
Holden, Ronald and
  Glenda Rote   Touring the Wine Country of Oregon   1982
                      Touring the Wine Country of Washington 1983
Holland, Tim   Behind the Label   1974
Holland, Tim and
  Arthur Bone   French Wines   1978
Holland, Vyvyan   Drink and be Merry   1967
Hollingworth, Jane   Collecting Decanters   1980
Holtgrieve, Don   The California Wine Atlas   1978
Hornickel, E.   The Great Wines of Europe   1965
Howkins, Ben   Rich Rare and Red (Port)   1982
Hudson, Horace B   California Vineyards   1902

Hudson, William	Wines of Italy	1888
Huggett, Henry E.V.	Rhenish, a Paper on Rhine Wines	1929
Hughes, Spike and Charmian Hughes	The Pocket Book of Italian Food and Wine	1986
Hughes, John	An Itinerary of Provence and the Rhone	1822
Hughes, William	The Complete Vineyard	1670
Hunt, Peter	Eating and Drinking; An Anthology for Epicures	1961
Hurley, Jon	Wine for Game and Fish - A Sporting Wife's Wine Companion	1986
Husenbeth, Frederick C.	A Guide for the Wine Cellar; or a Practical Treatise on the Cultivation of the Vine, and the Management of Different Wines Consumed in this Country (England)	1834
Husmann, George	An Essay on the Culture of the Grape in the Great West.....	1863
	The Cultivation of the Native Grape and Manufacture of American Wines	1866
	American Grape Growing and Wine Making. With Contributions from Well-Known Grape Growers etc.	1880
	Grape Culture and Wine Making in California A Practical Manual for the Grape-Grower and Wine-Maker	1888
Husmann, George Charles Frederick	Grape, Raisin and Wine Production in the US. USDA Yearbook	1902
Hutchinson, Peggy	Peggy Hutchinson's do's and dont's of Wine Making	1959
Hutchinson, Ralph B.	The California Wine Industry	1969
Hutchinson, Ralph and Sydney Blummer	The Williamson Act and Wine Growing in the Napa Valley	1970
Hutton, Isaac G.	The Vigneron; An Essay on the Culture of the Vine and Wine Making	1827
Hyams, Edward	The Grape Vine in England	1949
	Vineyards in England	1953
	Vin; The Wine Country of France	1960
	Dionysus, A Social History of the Wine Vine (Vitis Vinifera)	1969
Hyatt, Thomas Hart	Hyatt's Handbook of Grape Culture; or Why, Where, When and How to Plant a Vineyard,	

	Manufacture Wine ...California	1867
Jackisch, Philip	Modern Winemaking	1985
Jackson, Agnes	Fruit and Wine Farming in South Africa	1958
Jackson, David and		
Danny Schuser	Grape Growing and Wine Making; A	
	Handbook for Cool Climates	
	(New Zealand)	1981
Jackson, Joseph H. and		
James D.Hart	The Vine in Early California	1955
Jackson, Michael	Michael Jackson's Pocket Wine Book	1979
Jacob, Harry Ernest	Grape Growing in California	1950
Jacquelin, Louis and		
René Poulain	The Wines and Vineyards of France	1962
James,Margery K.	Studies on the Medieval English Wine Trade	
		1971
James, W. Bosville	Wine Duties Considered Financially and	
	Socially: Being a Reply to James Emerson	
	Tennent on Wine, its Taxation and uses..	1855
James, Walter	Barrel and Book; A Wine Maker's Diary	1949
	Wine in Australia; A Handbook	1952
	Nuts on Wine	1952
	What's What About Wine: An Australian	
	Wine Primer	1953
	A Word Book of Wine	1959
	Wine; a Brief Encyclopedia	1960
	Winegrowers Diary	1969
	The 1971 Wynn Winegrowers Diary and	
	Cellar Noteboke	1971
Jamieson, Ian	The Mitchell Beazley Pocket Guide to	
	German Wines	1984
	The Simon and Schuster Pocket Guide to	
	German Wines	1984
Jansen, Chris	Winelads of the Cape	1980
Jeffs, Julian	Sherry	1961
	Wine and Food of Portugal and Madeira	1965
	The Wines of Europe	1971
	The Dictionary of the World Wines	1973
	Little Dictionary of Drink	1973
Jobé, Joseph ed.	The Great Book of Wine	1970
Johnson, Frank	Professional Wine Reference	1977
Johnson, George W and		
Robert Errington	The Grape Vine; Its Culture, uses and	
	History	1847

Johnson, Grove   Practical Studies for the Winemaker, Brewer
                      and Distiller   1939
Johnson, George and
  Robert Errington   The Grape Vine; its Culture, uses and
                      History   1853
Johnson, Hugh   The Pan Book of Wine   1963
                      The Best of Vineyards is the Cellar 1965
                      Hugh Johnson's Modern Encyclopedia
                      of Wine   1966
                      Wine   1966
                      The World Atlas of Wine   1971
                      Pocket Encyclopedia of Wine   1977
                      Hugh Johnson's Wine Companion   1983
                      The Atlas of German Wines and Traveller's
                      Guide to theVineyards
                      Hugh Johnson's Pocket Book of Wine   1987
Johnson, Hugh. Ed.   The Pan Book of Wines   1983
Johnson, Samuel   Indulgence in Wine   1966
Johnson, Tom   The Story of Berry Bros. and Rudd, Wine
                      and Spirit Merchantsca.   ca. 1976
Jonas, Peter   Distiller's, Wine and Brandy Merchant's
                      Vade Mecum   1808
Jordan,Joseph V.   Simple Facts about Wines, Spirits, Liqueurs
                                                           1937
Jordan, Rudolf Jr.   Quality in Dry Wines Through Adequate
                      Fermentations   1911
Jorgensen, Alfred P.C.Practical Managemet of Pure Yeast. The
                      Application and Examination of Brewery,
                      Distillery and Wine Yeast   1936
                      Micro-Organisms and Fermentation   1848
Joske, Prue and Louise
Hoffmann   Wineries of Western Australia   1974
Joselyn, Maynard A.   A Technologist's View of the Calfifornia
                      Wine Industry   1974
Joslyn, Maynard A. and
Maynard A.Amerine Commercial Production of Dessert Wines 1941
                   Dessert, Appetizers and Related Flavoured
                   Wines; the Technology of their Production
                                                           1964
Joslyn Maynard A. and
  William V. Cruess   Elements of Wine Making   1934
                      Laboratory Examinations of Wines and
                      other Fruit Products   1934

146

Julien, André	The Topography of All the Known Vineyards (France)	1824
	Wine Merchant's Companion and Butler's Manual.	1825
Kafka, Barbara	American Food and Califoria Wine	1981
Karn, C.	Armagnac, Beaune. Bordeaux etc	1938
Kaufman, William I.	Wine and Cheese Tasting Party	1971
	Champagne	1973
	The Whole-World Wine Catalog	1978
	William I. Kaufman's Pocket Ebcyclopedia of California Wine	1981
	The Traveller's Guide to the Vineyards of North America	1980
	California Wine Drink Book	1982
	Encyclopedeia of American Wine, incl. Mexico and Canada	1984
	Pocket Encyclopedia of American Wineries East of the Rockies	1984
Kay, Billy and Cailean McLean	Knee Depp in Claret	1983
Keane, Eve	The Penfold Story (Australia)	1951
Kelly, Dr. Alexander	C.The Vine in Australia	1861
	Wine-Growing in Australia, and the Teaching of Modern Writers on Vine-Culture and Wine-Making	1867
Kelly, C.B.	The Grape in Ontario	1944
Kench, John and Phyllis Hands and David Hughes	The Complete Book of South African Wines	1983
Kew, Kenneth W.A.	In Search of Rarities: My Trip to European Vineyards	1963
Kilby, Kenneth	The Cooper and His Trade	1971
	The Village Cooper	1977
King, James	Australia may be an Extensive Wine-Producing Country	1857
Kirk, H.B.	Wine and Wine Drinkers of Today	1885
Kirton, John William	Intoxicating Drinks, their History and Mystery	1879
	A Glass of Foreign Wine (Claret, Port, Sherry)	1880
Klerk, W.A.de	The Wines of South Africa	1967
Knittel, John	Cyprus Wines from My Cellar	1933

148

Deborah Kenly and
Michael Topolos   Sonoma and Mendocin Wine Tour   1977
Laumer, William F. Jr. About Wines. Some Curiosties.........   1962
Launay, André   The Merrydown Book of Country Wines   1968
    Eat, Drink and be Happy   1970
Law, Ernest   King Henry VIII's Newe Wyne Seller at
    Hampton Court   1927
Lawrence, R. de
Treville, Sr.   Jefferson and Wine   1976
Laxer, Bernhard H.   Bern's Steak House Wine Book   1976
Layton, T.A   Choose Your Wine   1940
    Wine's My Line   1955
    Wines and Castles of Spain   1959
    Winecraft. The Encyclopaedia of Wines and
    Spirits   1961
    Wines of Italy   1961
    Modern Wines   1964
    Wines and Chateux of the Loire   1967
    Wines and People of Alsace   1970
Lee, Susan   Inexpensive Wine: A Guide to the Best   1974
Leedom, William S.   The Vintage Wine Book   1963
Leenaers, R.   The Mitchell Beazley Atlas of German
    Wines   1980
Leggett, Herbert B.   Early History of Wine Production in
    California   1941
Lagrand, N.E.   Champagne   1899
Leipoldt, C. Louis   300 Years of Cape Wine   1952
Lembeck, Harriet ed. Grossman's Complete Guide to Wines and
    Spirits   1983
Lesko, Leonard   King Tut's Wine Cellar   1977
Leslie, Francis C.   From Port to Port (Port Trade)   1946
Lester, Mary   Hand me that Corkscrew Bacchus   1973
Lewis, Robert A.   The Wines of Madeira   1968
Lichine, Alexis   The Wines of France   1969
    Encyclopedia of Wines and Spirits   1974
    Guide to the Wines and Vineyards of France
    1979
Lima, José Joaquim da
Costa   Port Wine   1938
    A Few Words about Port   1956
Lindemann, E.H.   The Practical Guide and Receipt Book for
    Distillers, Wine-Growers, Druggists,
    Manufacturers of Wines, Cordials....   1875

Lindemann, Richard H. Viticulture and Wine Economic and Social
                Life in the Thirteenth-Century 1975
Lindsey, William   Red Wine of Roussilon   1925
Littlewood, Joan   Milady Vine: The Autobiography of Baron
                Philippe de Rothschild   1984
Littlewood, Joan and
Edmund Penning-
Rowsell   Mouton - Baronne Phillipe   1981
Livingston-Learmonth
John and Melvyn
C. H. Masters   The Wines of the Rhone   1978
Lloyd, Frederick C.   The Art and Technique of Wine   1936
Lloyd, Paul   Concordance Among Wine Judges 1956
Loeb, O. and Terrence
Prittie   Moselle   1972
Loeb, Robert H. Jr.   How to Wine Friends and Affluent People 1965
Loftus, Simon   Anatomy of the Wine Trade   1985
Loftus, William Robert The Wine Merchant. A Familiar Treatise on
                the Art of Making Wine, with Introductory
                Remarks on Ancient and Modern Wines 1865
                The Wine and Spirit Merchant......   1870
Logan, Anne M.   Wine and Wine Cooking   1972
Logoz, Michel   Wine Label Design   1984
Lolli, Giorgio M.D.   Alcohol in Italian Culture
Long, Alistair   The Winemakers of the Clare Valley 1978
Longworth, Nicholas On the Cultivation of the Grape and
                Manufacture of Wine (USA)   1846
Lord, Tony   The New Wines of Spain   1988
Loubat, Alphonse   The American Vine Dresser's Guide   1827
Louberge, Leo   The Red and White: A History of Wine in
                France and Italy in the 19th Century 1978
Loyd, Rev. J.F.   Wine as a Beverage   1874
Lucas, Cyril   Making Sparkling Wine   1971
Lucia, Salvatore
Pablo M.D.   Dessert Wine: The Elexir of the Grape 1946
                Wine as Food and Medicine   1954
                Alcohol and Civilization   1963
                A History of Wine as Therapy   1963
                Wine and the Digestive System   1970
                Wine and Your Well Being   1971
                Wine Diet Cook Book   1974
Lucia Salvadore P
Pablo M.D. Ed.   Final Report of the National Study on the

	Medical Importance of Wine	1973
Lukas, Jan	The Book of Wine	1964
Lundy, Desmond	Leasure Winemaking	1978
Lutz, Henry Frederick	Viticulture and Brewing in the Ancient Orient	1922
Lyon, Alexander Victor	Problems of the Viticultural Industry	1924
Mabon, Mary	ABC of America's Wines	1942
MacArthur, William	Letters on the Culture of the Vine, Fermentation and the Management of the Wine Cellar	1844
MacCulloch, John	Remarks on the Art of Making Wine	1816
MacDonald, Barbara	Wine Cooking and Dining	1976
MacDonald, Kenneth and Throckmorton T.	Drink Thy Wine with a Merry Heart	1983
MacDougall, Katrina	Winery Buildings in South Australia	1980
MacGregor, James	Wine Making for All	1966
MacKenzie, Alexander	Califoria's Top 10 Wines	1983
Macquitty, Jane	Jane Macquitties Pocket Guide to Champagne and Sperkling Wines	1986
MacQuitty, Jane Ed.	Which? Wine Guide	1983
Madden, John	Shall We Drink Wine? A Physician's Study of the Alcohol Question	1899
Mahoney, John W.	Wines and Spirits: Labelling Requirements	1972
Mahoney, John W. (ed)	A Guide to Good Wine	1952
McDouall, Robin	Cooking with Wine	1968
Malet, William E.	The AustralianWine-Grower's Manual	1876
Manning, Sydney A.	A Handbook of the Wine and Spirit Trade	1947
	The Social Wine Guide	1952
Manning, Carol and Larry Roberts	Vineyards on the Mission Trail Book	1981
Marais, J.F.	The Reconstruction of Phylloxerised Vineyards	1893
Marcus, Irving H.	Dictionary of Wine Terms	1964
	How to Test and Improve Your Wine Judging Ability	1973
Margan, Frank	The Grape and I in NSW Australia	1969
	A Guide to the Hunter Valley	1971
	The Hunter Valley: Its People and History	1973
Marks, Robert, ed.	Wines: How, When and What to Serve	1934
Marrison, L.W.	Wines and Spirits	1957
	Wines for Everyone	1971

Garndener's Manual...... 1843
McFarland, Lynne. Ed.André L. Simon's Dictionary of Wines,
                Spirits and Liqueurs (Revised edition) 1983
McGregor, Marvin D. Grapes, Wine and Brandy (Review for
                1964-65). California 1964
McIndoe, David ed.   Chaman's New Zealand Grape Vine Manual
                or Plain Directions for Planting and
                Cultivating Vineyards for Wine Making 1862
McIver, L.L.   Kinda Vista Vineyards. Mission San José 1894
McKeown,Anthony G.Winemaking and Brewing without Tears 1973
McClean, James M.   Book of Wines 1934
McMullen, Thomas   Handbook of Wines 1852
McNeil, Arthus L.Rev.Mass Wine. Its Manufacter and Church
                Legislation 1938
McNeill, Florence M. The Scots Cellar, its Tradition and Lore 1958
McNulty, Henry   Drinking in Vogue 1978
                The Vogue Wine Book 1983
McPherson, John H. How to Choose and use Wine at Table 1968
McWilliam, D.M.   Wine Merchant's Recipes 1930
Mead, Peter B.   An Elementary Treatiseon American Grape
                Culture and Wine Making 1867
Meinhard, H.Heinrich German Wines 1971
                The Wines of Germany 1976
Meisel, Anthony and
 Shela Rosenzweig   On Wine 1983
Melville, John Robert Guide to California Wines 1968
Mendall, Seaton   Vineyard Practices for Finger Lake Growers
                                 1957
                Planting and Care of Young Vineyards in the
                Finger Lake Area of New York State 1960
Mendelson, Oscar A. The Earnest Drinker's Digest 1946
                The Earnest Drinker: A Short and Simple
                Accunt of Alcoholic Beverages 1950
                 Drinking with Pepys 1963
                The Dictionary of Drink and Drinking 1966
                From Cellar to Kitchen 1968
                Nicely, Thank You. A Frolic with some
                Synonyms 1971
Merdith, Joseph   Treatise on the Grape Vine 1876
Meredith, Ted   North West Wine: The Vinifera Wines of
                Oregon, Washington and Idaho 1980
Messenger, Elizabeth E.The Wine and Food Bank 1961
Mew, James and

John Aston	Drinks of the World	1892
Meyer, Otto E.	California Premium Wines and Brandies	1973
Michaels, Marjory	Stay Healthy with Wines. Natural Health and Beauty Secrets from the Vineyards	1981
Middleton, Scudder	Dining, Wining and Dancing in New York	1938
Milbourn, Thomas ed.	The Vintners´ Company, their Muniments, Plate and Eminent Members; with some account of the Ward of Vintry	1888
Milller, Mark	Wine, a Gentleman´s Game. The Story of Benmarl Vineyards (Hudson Valley)	1984
Milligan, David	All Colour Book of Wine	1974
Millon, Marc and Kim Millon	The Wine and Food of Europe	1982
	The Wine Roads of Europe	1983
Mills, Frederick C.	The Wine Guide; being Practical Hints on the Purchase and Management of Foreign Wines	1861
Mills, Samuel A.	The Wine Story of Australia	1908
Misch, Robert Jay	Quick Guide to Wine	1966
	Quick Guide to the Wines of all Americas	1977
Mitchell, John R.	Scientific Winemaking Made Easy	1969
Mitchell, Sir Thomas L.	Notes on the Culture of the Vine and the Olive and Methods of Making Wine and Oil in the Southern Parts of Spain	1849
Modi, Sir Jivanji Jamshedji	Wine Among the Ancient Persians: A Lecture delivered before the Self-Improvement Association - Bombay	1888
Mohr, Frederick	The Grape Vine . A Practical Treatise on its Management ... Wine Making. A Transaltion of Dr. Frederick Mohr´s work *Der Weinstock und der Wein.*	1867
Moisy, Robert	Beaujolais	1956
Montagne, Prosper	Larousse Gastronomique: The Encyclopedia of Food, Wine and Cookery	1961
Mooney, L.	Australian Wines: A Paper Read at the Special Meeting of the Victoria Chamber of Manufacturers	1883
Moore, Bernard	Wines of North America	1983
	Wines of the World	1984
Morel, Julian	Handbook of Wines and Beverages	1975
Morgan, Jefferson	Adventures in The Wine Country	1971
Morny, Claude, ed.	A Wine and Food Bedside Book	1972

Moro, Visconti G.	Somehting About Italian Wines: A Market	
	Guide	1958
Morrah, Patrick	André Simon - Goumet and Wine Lover	1987
Morrell, J.	An International Guide to Wines of the	
	World	1980
Morrel, J. and		
T.Stephenson	The Sunday Telegraph Good Wine Guide	1982
Morris, Denis	The French Vineyard	1958
	The Telegraph Guide to the Pleasures of	
	Wine	1972
	ABC of Wine	1977
Morris, Roger	The Genie in the Bottle; Unrravelling	
	Myths Abut Wine	1981
Morris, William	Praise of Wine	1958
Morton, Alexander	Just What You Want to Know About Wine	
		1890
Morton, Lucie, T.	Winegrowing in Eastern America	1985
Moser, Lenz	High Culture Systems.	
	Weibau einmal anders	1966
Mouraille, L.P.	Pactical Guide toTreatment of Wine in	
	English Cellars	1889
Mournetas, André		
and Henry Pelisser	The Vade Mecum of the Wine Lover	1953
Mowat, Jean. Ed.	Anthology of Wine	1946
Muench, Friedrich	School of American Culture- Vineyards	
	and the Production of Wine	1865
Muesch, John	A Treatise on the Use of Wine from	
	Religious and Organic Standpoints	1902
Muir, Augustus	Literature and Wine	1945
Muir, Augustus. Ed.	How to Choose and Enjoy Wine	1953
Mulder, Gerardus J.	The Chemistry of Wine	1857
Mulligan, Mary Ewing	Lets Throw an Italian Wine Tasting	1978
Munson, Thomas V.	Classification and Generic Synopsis of the	
	Wild Grapes of North America	1890
	Investigation and Improvement of American	
	Grapes at the Munson Experiment Station	
	from 1876-1900	1900
	Advantages of Conjoint Selection and	
	Hybridization and Limits of Usefulness	
	in Hybridization Among Grapes	1904
	Foundations of American Grape Culture	1909
Murphy, Brian	Vino	1969
Murphy, Dan F.	The Australian Wine Guide	1966

	What Wine is That? A Guide to Australian Wines	1973
	Dan Murphy´s Classification of Australian Wines	1974
	A Guide to Wine	1977
Murray, Samuel W.	Wines of the USA, How to Know and Choose them	1957
Murtric, W.M.	Report upon Statistics of Grape Culture and Wine Production in the US. for the Year 1880	1881
Muscatine, Doris and Maynard A. Amerine and Bob Thomson.Ed.	The Book of California Wine	1984
Muschamp, Michael	Wine and Winemakers of Australia	1977
Nelson, James Carmer	The Poor Person´s Guide to Cheap Wines	1977
	Everybody´s Guide to Wines under $5.	1983
Neuwirth, Art	The German Wines	1877
Newhall, Charles A.	The Vines of Northern America	1897
Newmark, A.	Tannin and its uses in Wine	1935
Nichol, Alexander	Wine and Vines in British Columbia	1983
Nicholas, Elizabeth	Madeira and the Canaries	1953
Niekerk, Tinus van	Wine Appreciation	1981
Niessen, Carl Anton	Report on the Vine Culure and the Wine Trade of Germany for the Years 1898-1900	1901
Norman, W.	More Fun with Wine	1973
North, Derek and Sally Brompton	How to Choose French Red Wines	1983
	How to Choose French White Wines	1983
Northey, Jo	Good Houskeeping Book of Wine	1974
Northover, Robin and Norma van Eck	The Feminine Touch: Wine and Food	1978
Nivitzky, Joseph W.D.	A Vineyard a Year	1984
Nowak, E. Carol and Vance A. Christian	Society of Wine Educators Guide to Wine	1980
Nury, F.S. and K.C. Fugelsang	The Winemaker´s Guide	1978
Nykanen, Lalli and H. Suomalainen	Aroma of Beer, Wine and Distilled Alcoholic Beverages	1983
Oldham, Charles F.	California Wines	1894
Oliver, Stuart	Wine Journeys	1949
Olken, Charles E. And		

156

Earl Singer and		
Norman Roby	The Connoisseur's Handbook of California	
	Wines	1980
Olmo, Harold Paul	A Survey of the Grape Industry of Western	
	Australia	1956
	Training and Trellising Grapevines for	
	Mechanical Handling: The Duplex System	1968
	Plant Genetics and New Grape Varieties	1974
Olney, Bruce	Liqueurs, Aperitifs and Fortified Wines	1972
Olney, Richard	Yquem	1985
Oppenheimer, Karl	Ferments and their Actions. Translated from	
	German	1901
Opperman, Diedrik J.	Spirit of the Vine (KWV South Africa)	1968
Ordish, George	Wine Growing in England	1953
	The Great Wine Blight (Phylloxera)	1972
	Vineyards in England and Wales	1977
Orffer, C.J. ed.	Wine Grape Cultivars in South Africa	1979
Osborn, John	Vineyards in America: With Remarks on	
	Temperance and Culture of Grape Vine in	
	the United States	1855
Osterman, Edmund	Wine and the Bottom Line	1980
Ott, Edward	From Barrell to Bottle	1963
	The Wines of rance	1980
	A Tread of Grapes: The Autovinography	
	of a Wine Lover	1982
Ough, Cornelius S.	Chemical, Physical and Microbiological	
	Stability of Wines and Brandies	1964
	Selection of Judges and Sensory Evaluation	
	of Wines	1964
Ough, Cornelius S. and		
Maynard A. Amerine	Effects of Temperature on Wine Making	1966
Ousback, Anders. Ed.	Words on Wine: A Collection of Quotations	
	Selected by Anders Ousback	1977
	The Australian Wine Browser	1979
Ozias, Blake	A Commentary on Wines	1934
	How the Modern Hostess Serves Wine	1934
	All About Wine	1967
Packman, W.Vance	Gentlemen's Own Guide to Wines	1902
	Wine and Spirit Manual and Packman's	
	Handy Agency List (London)	1903
Pacottet, Paul and		
L. Guittonneau	Wines of Champagne and Sparkling Wines	1930
Paguierre, M.	Classification and Description of the Wines	

157

	of Bordeaux	1928
Pama, Cor	Cape Wine Estates of South Africa	1979
Panarella, Giancarlo	Italian Wine and Brandy Buyers Guide	1975
Park, Robert M.D.	The Case of Alcohol: Or the Action of	
	Alcohol on Body and Soul	1909
Parker, Robert M. Jr.	Bordeaux: The Definitive Guide	1986
Paronetti, Lamberto	Chianti: A History of Florence and its Wines	
		1970
Parrack, Anne	Commonsense of Wine-Making	1978
Parrish, M.F.	The Story of Wine in California	1962
Pasteur, Louis	Studies on Fermentation	1879
Paterson, John	The Hamlyn Book of Wines	1975
	The International Book of Wines	1975
	Choos Your Wine	1980
	The Hamyn Pocket Dictionary of Wine	1980
Patton, William	The Laws of Fermentation and the Wines of	
	the Ancients	1871
	Bible Wines	1874
Payne, Brightham	The Story of Bacchus and Centennial	
	Souvenir	1876
Peabody, Richard	The Common Sense Book of Drinking	1931
Pearks, Gillian	Growing Grapes in Britain	1969
	Vinegrowing in Britain	1982
Peixetto, Ernest	A Bacchic Pilgrimiage. French Wine	1932
Pellegrini, Angelo	Wine and the Good Life	1965
Pellicot, André	The Wine and Winemaking in Southern	
	France	1868
Pellucci, Emanuele	Antinori: Vintners in Florence	1981
	Brunello di Montalcino	1981
Peninou, Ernest	Winemaking in California	1954
	A History of Orleans Hill Vineyard and	
	Winery of Arpad Harszthy and Company	1983
Penning-Rowsell,		
Edmund	Red, White and Rosé	1967
	The Wines of Bordeaux	1985
Penzer, Norman, M.	The Book of the Wine Label	1947
Peppercorn, David	Bordeaux	1982
	David Peppercorn's Pocket Guide to	
	The Wines of Bordeaux	1986
	Peppercorn, David, and	
Brian Cooper and		
Elwyn Blacker	Drinking Wine: A Complete Guide for	
	Buyer and Consumer	1979

Perell-Minetti, Antonio A Life of Wine Making   1975
Perold, Abraham IsaaK A Treatise on Viticulture (South Africa) 1927
Perry, Evan   Corksrews and Bottle Openers   1980
Peterson-Nedry, Judy Showcase Oregon Wineries   1981
Pettigrew, A.   The Vineyard at Castle Coch (Cardiff)   1884
Peynaud, Emile   Knowing and Making Wine   1984
Phillips, Dr.Gilbert The Appreciation of Wine   1950
Phillips, Marion. Ed. The Vineyard Almanac and Wine Gazzeteer
                                                               1980
Philpott, Don   The Vineyards of France   1987
Phipps, William   The Vintner's Guide....   1825
Pieroth, Kuno   The Great German Wine Book   1982
Platter, John   John Platter's Book of South African Wines
                                                               1980
Plimmer, R.H.A.   The Chemical Changes and Products
                     Resulting from Fermentation   1903
Pogash, Jeffrey   How to Read the Wine Label   1978
Pohren, D.E.   Adventures in Taste: The Wines and Folk
                     Foods of Spain   1972
Pongracz, D.P.   Practical Viticulture   1977
Ponsot, Maurice   Complete Year Book of French Quality
                     Wines   1945
Poprmilovic, Boris.Ed.Wines and Wine-Growing Districts of
                     Yugoslaia   1969
Postgate, Raymond   An Alphbet of Choosing and Serving Wine
                                                               1955
                     The Home Wine Cellar   1960
                     The Plain Man's Guide to Wine   1967
                     Portuguese Wine   1969
Potter, Mike   The Wines and Wineries of South Australia
                                                               1978
Poulter, Nick   Growing Vines   1972
                     Wines from Your Vines   1974
Poupon, Pierre and
 Forgeot, Pierre   A Book of Burgundy   1958
                     The Wines of Burgundy   1983
Pratt, James Norwood The Wine Bibber's Bible   1971
Prescott, Albert B. Chemical Examination of Alcoholic Liquors
                                                               1875
Prial, Frank J.   Wine Talk   1978
Price, Pamela VandykeCooking with Wine, Spirits, Beer and Cider
                                                               1959
                     France, a Food and Wine Guide   1966

	Winelovers Handbook	1969
	Eating and Drinking in France Today	1972
	Wines and Spirits	1972
	A Directory of Wines and Spirits	1974
	The Taste of Wine	1975
	Entertaining with Wine	1976
	Guide to the Wines of Bordeaux	1979
	Guide to the Wines of Champagne	1979
	Dictionary of Wines and Spirits	1980
	Understanding Wines and Spirits	1982
	Enjoying Wine: A Taster's Companion	1982
	The Century Companion to the Wines of Bordeaux	1983
	Alsace Wines	1984
	The Penguin Wine Book	1984
	Wine Lore, Legends and Traditions	1985
	Wine's Company; The entertaining Wine Course	1986
	French Vintage - A Personal Selection	1986
Price, Pamela Vandyke and Christopher Fielden	Alsace Wines and Spirits	1984
Prince, William R.	A Treatise on the Vine. History from Earliest Ages to the Present Day	1830
Puisais, J.	Initiation into the Art of Wine Tasting	1974
Purser, J. Elizabeth	The Winemakers (Washington and Oregon)	1977
Quimme, Peter	The Signet Book of American Wine	1975
Raelson, Jeffrey	Getting to Know German Wines	1979
Rainbird, George M.	The Pocket Book of Wine	1963
	The Wine Handbook	1964
	Sherry and the Wines of Spain	1966
	An Illustrated Guide to Wine	1983
Ramey, Bern C.	Pocket Book of Wines	1970
	The Great Wine Grapes and the Wines they Make	1977
Ramsden, Eric	James Busby: The Prophet of Australian Viticulture and British Resident at New Zealand (1833-40)	1941
	Busby of Waitangi - Resident of New Zealand	1974
Rankine, Bryce C.	Observations on Wine Making and Wine Research in France, Germany, Switzerland	

	and California...	1967
	Wines and Wineries of the Barossa Valley	1971
Ranne, Williams F.	Wines of Ontario	1978
Ray, Cyril	Introduction to Wines	1960
	The Wines of Italy	1966
	Bollinger	1971
	Fide et Fortitudine. The Story of a Vineyard:	
	Langoa-Leoville Barton 1821-1971	1971
	The House of Warre 1670-1970	1971
	The Story of Ch. Lafite-Rothschild	1971
	Mouton-Rothschild	1971
	The Wines of France	1976
	The Wines of Germany	1977
	Cyril Ray´s Book of Wine	1978
	Ruffino: The Story of a Chianti	1978
	Lickerish Limerics. -Drawings by Charles	
	Moseley	1979
	Ray on Wine	1979
	The New Book of Italian Wines	1982
	Robert Mondavi of the Napa Valley	1984
Ray, Cyril. Ed.	The Compleat Inbiber 1-12	1956-1971
	Vintage Tales - An Anthology of Wine and	
	Other Intoxications	1984
Ray, Cyil & Elizabeth	Wine with Food	1975
Ray, George	The French Wines	1965
Read, Jan	The Wines of Spain and Portugal	1973
	Guide to the Wines of Spain	1977
	The Wines of Portugal	1982
	The Wines of Spain	1982
	The Century Companion to the Wines of	
	Spain and Portugal	1983
	The Pocket Guide to Spanish Wines	1983
	The Mirchell Beazley Pocket Guide to	
	Spanish Wines	1983
	The Mitchell Beazley Pocket Guide to	
	Wines of Spain	1983
	The Wines of Rioja	1984
Reay-Smith, John	Discovering Spanish Wines	1976
Redding, Cyrus	A History and Description of Modern Wines	1836
	Every Man his own Butler	1839
	French Wines and Vineyards; and the Way	
	to Find them	1860

Reed, Myrtle	Master of the Vineyard	1910
Reed, Stan	The Wine World at a Glance	1969
Reichert, Alfred	The Future of German Viticulture in the ECM (European Common Market)	1960
Reid, J.G.S.	The Cool Cellar	1969
Renwick, Cyril	A Study of the Wine in the Hunter Region of N.S.W.	1977
Repetto, Victor and Sydney J. Block	Perspectives on California Wines	1976
Rhodes, Anthony	Princes of the Grape: Great Wine Makers Through the Ages	1975
Ridgway, Judy	Running Your Own Wne Bar	1984
Riker, Douglas H.	The Wine Book of Knowledge	1934
Riley, Norman and Hugo Dunn-Meynell	Wine Record Book	1968
Rixford, Emmet H.	The Wine Press and the Cellar. A Manual for the Winemaker and the Cellar-Man	1883
Robards, Terry	Wine Cellar Journal	1974
	The New York Times Book of Wine	1976
	California Wine Label Album	1981
	A Votre Santé. A Complete Guide to French Wines	1982
Roberge, Earl	Napa Wine Country	1975
Roberts, Ivor	Great Australian Wines	1969
Roberts, Ivor and Douglas Baglin	Australian Wine Pilgrimage	1969
Roberts, Jeremy and Joisé Northey. Ed.	The Wines of the World	1974
Robertson, George	Port	1978
Robertson, Jean and Andrew Robertson	Food and Wine of the French Provinces	1968
Robinson, James	The Whole Art of Making British Wines	1848
	The Art and Mystery of Making British Wines, Cider and Perry.....With Directions for the Management of Foreign Wines and Spirituous Liquors	1865
Robinson, Jancis	The Wine Book: A Straight-Forward Guide to Buying and Drinking Better Wines for less Money	1979
	The Great Wine Book	1982
	Masterglass. A Practical Course on Wine Tasting	1983
	How to Choose and Enjoy Wine	1984

Robinso, Jancis. Ed.	Which? Wine Guide	1981
Robotti, Peter and Frances Robotti	Key to Gracious Living: Wine and Spirits	1972
Robson, Edgar I.	A Wayfarer to French Vineyards	1928
Roger, J.R.	The Wines of Bordeaux	1960
Rollat, Edouard	Wine Guide and Cocktail Book	1934
Rolli, Otto Christian	Wine for Home and Medicinal Use	1933
Roncarati, Bruno	D.O.C. The New Image for Italian Wies	1971
	Viva Vino, D.O.C.Wines of Italy	1976
Rook, Alan	The Diary of an English Vineyard	1969
Roos, L	Wine Making in Hot Climates	1900
Roose, Samuel	New and Complete Treatise on Ullaging.	1832
	Wine and Spirit Dealer's Guide	1835
Rootes, Nicholas	The Drinker's Companion	1987
Roper, Elmo	A Study of People's Attitudes Toward and usage of Wine	1955
Rose, John	The English Vineyard Vindicated	1666
Rossati, Guido	Descriptive Accunt of the Wine Industry of Italy	1888
Rossi, F.	An Investigation into the Vine Industry of Cyprus	1956
Rothschild, Philippine de and Jean-Pierre de. Beaumarchais	Mouton Rothschild Paintings for the Labels	1983
Roux, Michel Pierre	A Guide to the Vineyards and Chateaux of Bordeaux	1972
Roux, Michel Pierre and Pierre Poupon and Pierre Forgeot	A Guide to the Vineyards and Domains of Burgundy	1973
Rowe, Percy	The Wines of Canada	1970
Rowe, Vivian	French Wines - Ordinary and Extraordinary	1972
Rudd, Hugh R.	Hocks and Moselles	1935
Ruland, Wilhelm	Legends of the Rhine	------
	The Finest Legends of the Rhine	------
Russell, Mark. Ed.	The Paragon of Wines and Spirits	1973
Sabin, A	Wine and SpiritMerchant's Accounts	1904
Saint Pierre, Louis de	Art of Planting and Cultivating the Vine and also of Making, Fining and Preserving Wines According to the most Celebrated Wine-Counties in France	1772

Saintsbury, George	Notes on a Cellar Book	1920
	A Scrap Book	1922
	A Second Scrap Book	1923
	The Last Scrap Book	1924
	Professor of Taste	1936
Salisbury-Jones, Sir Guy	A Short History of Hambledon Wine	ca. 1967
	Wine Growing in Britain (Royal Society of Arts Journal)	1973
Sanceau, Elaine	The British Factory (House) Oporto	1970
Sandeman, George	Port and Sherry	1955
Sanders, Bob and Seb Jensen	The Vineyards of the Hunter Valley	1971
Sanderson, William	A Few Practical Remarks on the Medicinal Effect of Wine and Spirits...	1799
Sarles, John	ABC's of Italian Wines	1981
Sarvis, Shirley	American Wines and Wine Cooking	1973
Saunders, Peter	A Guide to New Zealand Wine	1976
	Wine Label Language	1976
Schenk, Henry A. Ed.	The New Medical Wine Book	1922
Schneider, Steven J.	The International Album of Wine	1977
Scholz, Merve	Wine Country	1970
Schoonmaker, Frank	The Complete Wine Book	1934
	Distinguished American Wines	1946
	Dictionary of Wines	1952
	Vintage Chart 1945-1954	1954
	The Wines of Germany	1956
	German Wines	1957
	Frank Schoonmaker's Encyclopedia of Wine	1964
	Vintages of the Nineteen-Sixties: 1959-1967	1968
Scott, Dick	Winemakers of New Zealand	1965
Scott, James Maurice	The Vineyards of France	1950
	The Man Who Made Wine	1953
Searle, Ronald	The Illustrated Winespeak. Ronald Searl's Wicked World of Wine Tasting	1983
	Something in the Cellar: Ronald Searle's Wonderful World of Wine	1983
Seely, James	Great Bordeaux Wines	1986
Seldon, Philip	The Vintage Magazine Consumer Guide to Wine	1983
Seldon, Philip. Ed.	The Great Wine Chateaux of Bordeaux	1975
Selivanova, Nina	Dining and Wining in Old Russia	1933

Selllers, Charles	Oporto, Old and New; being a Historical Record of the Port Wine Trade, and a Tribute to British Commercial Enterprise in the North of Porugal	1899
Seltman, Charles	Wine in the Ancient World	1957
Serjeant, Richard	A Man May Drink	1964
Serlis, Harry G.	Wine in America	1972
Seward, Desmond	Monks and Wine	1979
Shand, Phillip Morton	A Book of Wine	1925
	Bacchus; or Wine Today and Tomorrow	1927
	A Book of French Wines	1928
	A Book of other Wines than French	1929
	A Book of Food (and Wine)	1930
Shanken, Marvin. Ed.	The Wine Spectator Guide to Selected Wines	1985
Shatman, Fay	The Taste of France. A Dictionary of French Food and Wine	1982
Sharp, Andrew	Wine Taster's Secrets, the Consumer's Guide to Wine Tasting	1981
Sharp, William J.	Wine: How to Develop Your Taste and Get Your Money's Worth	1976
Shaver, Gordon O.	Wines and Liquors from the Days of Noah.	1939
Shaw, Henry	The Vine and Civilization	1984
Shaw, Peter, M. D.	The Juice of the Grape; or Wine Preferable to Water	1724
Shaw, Thomas George	Wine, the Vine, and the Cellar	1863
	The Wine Trade, and its History	1851
	Wine in Relation to Temperence	1854
Shepherd, C.W.	Wines, Spirits and Liqueurs	1971
Siegel, Hans	Guide to the Wines of Germany	1978
Simon, André L.	The History of the Champagne Trade in England	1905
	The History of the Wine Trade in England Vols. I, II and III	1906/9
	The Wine Trade of England: A Lectur at Vintner'Hall	1911
	Alcohol and the Human Body	1912
	The Art of Making Wine. A Lecture at Vintners' Hall	1912
	In Vino Veritas	1913
	Claret and Sauternes	1919
	Wine and Spirits, the Connouisseur's Textbook	1919

        8. Hocks and Moselles
        9. Brandy
     10. Rum
     11. Madeira
     12. Italy
     13. Yugoslavia
     14. Switzerland and Luxembourg
     15. California
     16. Alsace, Arboise and Loire
     Valley
     17. The Rhone, Provence,
     Languedoc and Roussilon 1950/51

Simon, André L. and Ronald Avery	Talking of Wine	1962
Simon André L. and Elizabeth Craig	Madeira Wine, Cakes and Sauce	1933
Simon, André L. and S.F. Hallgarten	Great Wines of Germany and its Famed Vineyards	1963
Simson, Sally	Wine of Good Hope	1983
Singleton, Vernon L.	Phenolic Substances in Grapes and Wine and their Significance	1969
Sitwell, Sacheveral	Portugal and Madeira	1954
Slessor, Kenneth	The Grapes ar Growing: The Story of Australian Wine.	1963
Smeed, T.	The Wine Merchant's Manual. A Treatise the Fining, Preparation of Finings and General Managemnt of Wine Consumed in this Country (England)	1845
Smith, Joanna	The New English Vineyard	1979
Sneesby, Norman	A Vineyard in England	1977
Speechley, William	A Treatise on the Culture of the Vine, Vineyards etc	----- 1789
Speight, Robert	The Companion Guide to Burgundy	1975
Spinola, Oberto	The Martini Museum of the History of Wine Making	-----
Spooner, Alden J.	The Cultivation of American Grape Vines and Making of Wine	1846
Spurrier, Steven	The Concise Guide to French Country Wines	1982
	French Fine Wines	1984
	Guide to French Wines	1984
	Wine Cellar Book	1986

Spurrier, Steven and	
Michael Dovaz	Academie du Vin Complete Wine Course	1983
Stanislawski, Dan	Landscape of Bacchus, the Vine in Portugal	
		1970
Steel, Anthony	The Custom of the Room or Early Wine	
	Books of Christ's College Cambridge	1949
Stevenson, Robert L.	Napa Wine	1974
Stevenson, Tom	Champagne	1986
Stockley, C.S.	Medically, is Wine Just Another Alcoholic	
	Beverage? Proceedings of the Wolf Blass	
	Foundation International Wine and Health	
	Conference	1996
Stockley, Tom	Winery Trails of the Pacific Northwest	1977
	Winery Tours in Oregon	1978
Stokes, Alan	Vineyards of North East Victoria	1970
Storm, John	An Invitation to Wines; an Informal Guide	
	to the Selection, Care and Enjoment of	
	Domestic and European Wines	1955
Srett, Julian L.	Wines, their Selection, Care and Serice	1933
Sullivan, Charles	Like Modern Edens; Winegrowing, in	
	Santa Clara Valley and Santa Cruz	
	Mountains 1798-1981	1982
Sutcliffe, Serena	The Wines of France	1967
	The Wine Drinker's Handbook	1982
	Serene Sutcliffe's Pocket Guide to	
	The Wines of Bugundy	1986
Surcliffe, Serena. Ed.	André Simon's Wines of the World	1981
	The Art of the Wine Maker	1981
	Great Vineyards and Winemakers	1982
Sutherland, G.	The South Australian Vinegrowers's	
	Manual. A Practical Guide to the Art of	
	Viticulture in South Australia	1892
Suttor, George	The Culture of the Grape-Vine, and the	
	Orange, in Australia - with observations of	
	the Vineyards of France and the Rhine - and	
	Extracts Concerning all the Most Celebrated	
	Wines	1843
Symington, J. D.	Port Wine (Oporto)	1954
Tail, Geoffrey M.	Practical Handbook on Port Wine	1925
	The Art of Appreciating Wine	1931
	Port: From the Vine to the Glass	1936
Taylor, Allan	What Everybody Wants to Know About	
	Wine	1934

Taylor, Greyton H.	Treasury of Wine and Wine Cookery	1963
Taylor, Howard	The Handbook of Wines and Liquors	1933
Taylor, Sally	Cakifornia Wine Maps and Directory	1983
Taylor, Sidney, B.	Wine, Wisdom and Whimsy	1969
Taylor, Walter S.	Living Wine Grapes of the Finger Lakes, an Ampelography	1972
Teiser, Ruth and Catherine Harroun	Wine Making in California	1982
Tennent, Sir James E.	Wine, Its Use and Taxation	1855
Theron, Christian J. and Charles Niehaus	Wine Making	1948
Thiebaut, de Bernaud	The Vine-Dresser's Theoretical and Practical Manual, or the Art on Cultivating the Vine: and Making Wine, Brandy and Vinegar	1829
Thompson, Bob	The Pocket Encyclopedia of California Wines	1980
Thompson, Bob. Ed	California Wine Country	1971
	California Wine	1973
Thompson, Bob and Hugh Johnson	The California Wine Book	1976
Thompson, William	A Practical Treatise on the Cultivation of the Grape Vine	1862
Thorpy, Frank	Wine in New Zealand	1983
	New Zealand Wine Gude	1976
Thudichum, John L.W.	Report on the Chemical Analysis of Wines of the Pure Wine Association Limited	1871
	On Wines, their Production, Treatment and Use.	1873
	The Aasthetical use of Wine and its Use upon Health	1884
	Alcoholic Drinks	1884
Thudichum, Joh. L.W. and A. Dupré	A Treatise on the Origin, Nature, and Varieties of Wine: Being a Complete Manual of Viticulture and Oenology	1872
	A Treatise on Wines : Their origin, Nature, and Varieties, with Practical Directions for Vitculture and Vinification	1894
Tigney, Frederick	Wine Roads of France	1977
Tigney, Nancy	Wine Roads of Italy	1977
Timbrel, Tilly	The Winemaker's Dining Book: Week by Week Menus for Winemakers	1972
Timothy, Brother	The Christian Brothers as Winemakers	1974

Tod, H.M.	Vine-Growing in England	1911
Todd, William	A Handbook of Wine; How to Buy, Serve, Store, and Drink it	1922
	Port: How to Buy, Serve, Store and Drink it	1926
Tomes, Robert	The Champagne Country	1867
Tonta, Geoff	The Butler´s Guide to the Making of Wines, Beer, and Liqeuors in a Gentleman´s Cellar	1977
Topolos, Michael and Betty Dobson	California Wineries: Napa Valley	1975
	Napa Valley Wine Tour	1978
Torbert, Harold C.	The Complete Wine and Food Cookbook	1972
Torbertm Harold and Frances Torbert	The Book of Wine	1972
Torres, Miguel A.	The Vine and Wines of Spain	1982
Tovey, Charles	Wine and Wine Countries: A Record and Manual forWine Merchants and Wine Consumers	1862
	Champagne: Its History, Manufacture...... with some Remarks on Wine and Wine Merchants	1870
	Wine Revelations	1880
	Wit, Wisdomand Morals Distilled from Bacchus	1878
Treber, Grace	World Wine Almanac and Wine Atlas - a Complete Guide and Catalogue of Wine Labels	1976
Tritton, Suzanne M.	Grape Growing and Wine Making, including the Vintner´s Calendar	1949
	Grape Growing and Wine-Making from Grapes and other Fruits	1951
	Successful Wine and Beer Making	1960
	Wine Making from Pulps, Fruit and Concentrates	1963
	Tritton´s Guide to Better Wine and Beer Making for Beginners	1965
Tudor, Dean	Wine, Beer and Spirits	1975
Tuor, Conrad	Wine and Food Handbook	1977
Turner, Anthony and Christopher Brown	Burgundy. Its Wines, Food Architecture and History	1977
Turner, Bernard C	Behind the Wine List	1968

	Growing your Own Wine	1977
	The Winemaker's Encyclopaedia	1979
Turner, William	A New Boke of the Natures and Porperties	
	of all Wines that are Commonly used here in	
	England, with a Confutation of an Errour of	
	some Men, that Holde, that Rhennish and	
	other Small White Wines ought not to be	
	Drunk of them that either Haue, or are in	
	Daunger of the Stone...	1568
Valaer, Peter J.	Wines of the World	1950
Valente-Perfeito, J.C.	Let's Talk about Port	1948
Van Buren, J.	The Scuppernong Grape: Its History and	
	Mode of Cultivation, with a short Treatise	
	on the Manufactore of Wine from it.	1871
Varounis, George	An Introduction to French Wines and Spirits	
		1933
Verdier, G.	History of Wine	1933
Viala, P and Viala L.	American Vines	1901
Veronelli, Luigi	The Wines of Italy	1950
Vidoudez, Michael	The Great Wines of the World	1982
Villanis, P.	Theoretical and Practical Notes upon	
	Wine-Making, and the Treatment of Wines,	
	Especially Applied to Australian Wines	1884
Vine, Richard P.	Commercial Winemaking, Processing and	
	Controls	1981
Vispre, François A.	A Dessertation on the Growth of Wine in	
	England: to Serve as an Introduction to a	
	Treatise on the Method of Cultivating	
	Vineyards in a Coutry from wich they seem	
	entirely Eradicated: and Making from them	
	Good Substantial Wine	1786
Vitucci, Gino	Overseas Study Tour to Observe and Study	
	Wine Grape Growng and Wine Industry in	
	Europe and USA	1976
Vizetelly, Ernest A.		
and Vicetelli Arthur	The Wines of France with a Chapter on	
	Cognac and Table Waters	1908
Vizetelly, Henry	The Wines of the World Characterized and	
	Classed	1875
	Facts about Sherry	1876
	Facts about Chamagne and other	
	Sparkling Wines	1879
	How Champagne was first Discovered and	

	how the Wine is now Produced	1879
	Facts about Port and Medeira	1880
	A History of Champagne	1882
	Glances Back through Seventy Years: Autobiographical and other Reminiscences	1893
Wagenyoord, James	The Doubleday Wine Companion	1983
Wagner, Philip M.	American Wines and how to Make them	1933
	Wine Grapes; their Selection, Cultivation and Enjoyment	1937
	A Wine-Grower's Guide	1945
	American Wines and Wine Making	1956
	Grapes into Wine; a Guide to Winemaking in America	1976
Walch, G. Ed	A Glass of Champagne: The Story of the King of Wines with a Description of its Preparation, Mode of Storage, and Distribution, as Carried out by Messrs. Krug and Company	1885
Waldo, Myra	The Pleasures of Wine	1963
Walker, A.	Prospects for Wine Grape Production in Shire of Kaniva (Australia)	1971
Walker, G. J.	1001 Questions and Answers about Wine	1976
Walker, James	Hints to Consumers of Wine: On the Abuse which Enhances the Price of that Article	1802
Wallace, E.	The Game of Wine	1977
Walls, Bill	Southern Vineyards Sketchbook (Australia)	1976
Walter, Frederick	Wine and Wine Making	1938
Ward, Ebenezer	The Vineyards and Orchards of South Australia	1862
Ward, H.W.	The Book of the Grape	MCMI
Warner, Charles K.	The Winegrowers of France and the Government since 1875	1960
Warner, Ferdinando	A Full and Plain Account of Gout..	1768
Warre, James	Past, Present and Possible Future State of the Wine Trade.	1823
Waserman, Sheldon and Pauline Wasserman	The Wines of Italy	1976
	The Wines of the Cotes du Rhone	1977
	White Wines of the World	1978
	Guide to Fortified Wines	1983
	Sparkling Wine	1984
Waterson, M.J.	The U.K. Market for Beers, Wines and	

	Spirits 1977 to 1985	1978
Watney, Bernard and Homer D. Babidge	Corksrews for Collectors	1981
Watt, Alexander	Bordeaux and its Wines	1957
Waugh, Alec	Merchants of Wine ; being a Centenerary Account of the House of Gilbey	1957
	In Praise of Wine and Certain Noble Spirits	1959
	Wines, Spirits from the Time-Life Book Series "Foods of the World"	1969
Waugh, Evelyn	Wine in Peace and War	1947
Waugh, Harry	Bacchus on the Wing: A Wine Merchant's Travelogue	1966
	The Changing Face of Wine	1968
	Diary of a Winetaster. Recent Tastings of French and California Wines	1972
	Wine Taster's Choice; the Years of Hysteria, Tastings of French, California and German Wines	1974
	Harry Waugh's Wine Diary Vol. 6	1975
	Harry Waugh's Wine Diary Vol.7	1976
	Harry Waugh's Wine Diary Vol. 8	1978
	Harry Waugh's Wine Diary Vol. 9	1981
	Harry Waugh's Wine Diary 1982-1986	1987
	Pick of the Bunch	1970
Waverman, Luey	The Panny Pinchers's Wine Guide	1983
Webber, Alaxander	Wine. A Series of Notes on this Valuable Product	1889
Weihold, Rudolph	Vivat Bacchus: A History of Wine and its Viticulture	1976
Weinman, J.	Manual of the Industry of Sparkling Wines, description of the Chemical and Practical Customerily used in Champagne	1917
Welby, Thomas Earle	The Cellar Key	1933
Weld, Charles Richard	Notes on Burgundy	1869
West, William	Wine and Spirit Adulterations Unmasked	1827
Wetmore, Charles A.	Treatise on Wine Production	1894
Wheatley, Dennis Y.	Drink and Ink, the Memoirs of Dennis Wheatley (Wine Merchant)	1949
	1749-1949: The Seven Ages of Justerini's	1949
Whitaker, Tobias	The Tree of Humane Life, or, the Blood of the Grape. Proving the Possibility of Life	

	from Infancy to ExtremeOld Age without Sickness by the use of Wine	1638
White, O.E.D.	A Guide to Australian Wine	1972
Whitington, E.	South Australian Vintage 1903	1903
Whitworth, Eric W.	Wine Labels	1979
Wildman, Frederick S.	A Wine Tour of France	1972
Wile, Julius. Ed.	Frank Schoonmaker'sEncyclopedia of Wine	1978
Williams, C.D.	A Simple Guide to Andalusia (Wine)	1926
Williams, Darcy	The Manufacture of Flor Sherry	1943
Williams, G.C.	Shakespeare's Wine Book. William Turner's New Boke of Nature and Propereties of Wine	1923
Wilson, Robert Forest	How to Wine and Dine in Paris	1930
Winkler, Albert Julius	Viticultural Research at the University of California, Davis	1973
	General Viticulture	1975
Winston, Basil J. and Ross Firestone	Getting into Wine	1975
Woodin, G.B.	All You need to know about Wine	1969
Woon, Basi	The Big and Little Wines of France Vol.1	1972
	The Big and Little Wines of France Vol.2	1976
Worth, William M.D.	A New Art of Making Wines, and Brandy, and other Spirits....	1691
Wyndham, Guy R.C.	Port:; from Grape to Glass	1947
	Sherry from Grape to Glass	1949
Wynn, Allan	The Fortunes of Samuel Wynn. Winemaker, Humanist,and Zionist	1969
Yapp, Robin and Judith Yapp	Vineyards and Vignerons	1979
Yeadon, Anne and David Yeadon	Wine Tasting in California	1973
Yorke-Davies, Nathaniel Edward	Wine and Health. How to Enjoy Both	1909
Youell, Tessa and George Kimbal	The Pocket Guide to French Food and Wine	1985
Young, Alan	Australian Wines and Wineries	1983
Younger, William	Gods Men and Wine	1966
Youngman-Carter	Drinking Bordeaux	1966
	Drinking Burgundy	1966
	Drinking Champage and Brandy	1968

Yoxall, Harry W.   Women and Wine   1954
                    The Wines of Burgundy   1968
                    The Enjoyment of Wine   1972
Zauner, Phyllis   Wine Country: The Sonoma and Napa
                      Valleys   1983
Zupan, Walter   Viennese Heurigen Handbook   1959

www.ingramcontent.com/pod-product-compliance
Lightning Source LLC
Chambersburg PA
CBHW052046090426
42739CB00010B/2059